D0517588

PAINTING A
World of Enchantment

Bobbie Takashima

NORTH LIGHT BOOKS
CINCINNATI, OHIO
www.artistsnetwork.com

ACKNOWLEDGMENTS

*This book was made possible through the love and support
of very special people:*

*My deepest gratitude to Kathy Chapman, a longtime friend,
for all you've done to allow me the time needed to work on this book.
I couldn't have done it without you.*

*Many thanks to the people at North Light Books
for your guidance, patience and cooperation.*

*To Royal & Langnickel Brush Manufacturing,
thank you for furnishing me with your fine line of brushes.*

*Thanks to Donna and Max Crews at Country Pleasures
for providing the many unique, quality wood surfaces found in this book.*

*To all my painting friends at home and abroad.
Your enthusiasm, encouragement and input keep me creative.
My deepest thanks to you all.*

DEDICATION

To my family

Who gave me wings

To follow my heart

To fulfill my dreams

I love you

Painting a World of Enchantment. Copyright © 2002 by Bobbie Takashima. Manufactured in China. All rights reserved. The patterns and drawings in this book are for the personal use of the decorative painter. By permission of the author and publisher, they may be either hand-traced or photocopied to make single copies, but under no circumstances may they be resold or republished. It is permissible for the purchaser to paint the designs contained herein and sell them at fairs, bazaars and craft shows. No other part of this book may be reproduced in any form or by any electronic or mechanical means including information storage and retrieval systems without permission in writing from the publisher, except by a reviewer, who may quote brief passages in a review. Published by North Light Books, an imprint of F&W Publications, Inc., 4700 Galbraith Rd., Cincinnati, Ohio, 45236. (800) 289-0963. First edition.

06 05 04 03 02   5 4 3 2 1

Library of Congress Cataloging-in-Publication Data
Takashima, Bobbie.
    Painting a world of enchantment / Bobbie Takashima.
        p. cm.
    Includes index.
    ISBN 1-58180-074-6 (alk. paper)— ISBN 1-58180-075-4 (alk. paper)
    1. Painting. 2. Decoration and ornament. 3. Handicraft. I. Title.

TT385 .T35 2002
745.7'23—dc21   2001044871

Edited by Maureen Mahany Berger and Heather Dakota
Production coordinated by Kristen D. Heller
Designed by Joanna Detz
Page layout by Linda Watts
Photographed by Christine Polomsky

Metric Conversion Chart

TO CONVERT	TO	MULTIPLY BY
Inches	Centimeters	2.54
Centimeters	Inches	0.4
Feet	Centimeters	30.5
Centimeters	Feet	0.03
Yards	Meters	0.9
Meters	Yards	1.1
Sq. Inches	Sq. Centimeters	6.45
Sq. Centimeters	Sq. Inches	0.16
Sq. Feet	Sq. Meters	0.09
Sq. Meters	Sq. Feet	10.8
Sq. Yards	Sq. Meters	0.8
Sq. Meters	Sq. Yards	1.2
Pounds	Kilograms	0.45
Kilograms	Pounds	2.2
Ounces	Grams	28.4
Grams	Ounces	0.04

ABOUT THE AUTHOR

A love of arts and crafts has been a part of me since early childhood. Tagging along with my mother to paint class and other craft classes nurtured and inspired the artist in me.

My first formal art classes began in 1960 at a local studio. From that year to this, I've studied with many decorative artists who have helped to educate me and to inspire me to pursue my love of art.

I do not hold any titles or art degrees but choose to let my work speak for the years of self-study and experience in the field. My passion is my love of designing, painting, teaching and self-study.

I opened Country Keepsakes Folk Art Studio in 1985. Nationally recognized teachers and I conduct seminars and classes there. Students come from near and far: Japan, Australia, England and across the United States.

I have authored four other painting books, along with numerous articles for magazines, which include *Decorative Artist's Workbook, Artist's Journal*, Chroma Acrylic's publication, Royal & Langnickel publications and a number of Japanese decorative art magazines. I have also had the pleasure of appearing on Japanese TV.

There are currently more than a hundred of my pattern packets available and distributed worldwide. Travel teaching my artwork across the United States, Japan, Australia, England, Scotland and Canada has fulfilled a lifelong dream to see the world. It is a joy to realize this dream and to know that wherever this art takes me, there is a common bond with others through painting.

Along with the travel teaching, I have taught and exhibited my artwork at twelve national conventions and six mini-conventions since 1979.

When not on the road teaching, I may be found at my studio, Country Keepsakes, located at 340 West Twenty-sixth St., Suite D, National City, CA 91950.

Please visit my Web site at www.BobbieArtStudio.com or e-mail me at BTFrogs@aol.com. I would love to hear from you. Any inquiries regarding seminars or book and packet projects are welcome.

Enjoy your journey of art!

Toadally,

Bobbie

Table of Contents

Getting Started

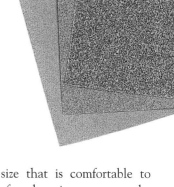

TECHNIQUES

The painting techniques of the decorative artist today have expanded to the far reaches of the imagination. The brushes, pigments and mediums currently available to artists have also expanded our ability to express our imaginations. Life is good!

The painting techniques and products used for the projects in this book are few by comparison but they are also my favorites. There is a combination of techniques to create depth, texture and a variety of visual effects.

Brush Sketching

The brush sketching technique is an old canvas painting technique which I have adapted for decorative painting. Painting over the graphite pattern lines with paint and a brush helps to define the pattern but provides a more "painterly" appearance. The edges of the pattern are a bit softer this way. Also, a better variety of line widths can be achieved in order to add more or less paint to a given area.

Depending on the color used, this brush sketching can be the first step in the shading process or it can be executed in another hue desired in the design. Sometimes the brush sketching shows through the overpainting as a detail line. It is very versatile.

Drybrushing

Drybrushing may produce a coarse to very fine textural effect depending upon the type of brush, amount of pigment in the brush, medium and amount of medium mixed with the pigment and the hand pressure applied to all of the preceding.

The dry-brush technique produces an open, or broken, coverage of pigment, allowing underlying pigment to be visible. The visual effects of texture and color are unlimited. I like the soft edges that are produced, especially when contrasted with hard edges.

All of the projects in the book have some degree of drybrushing. Some begin with dry-brushed backgrounds (refer to the Frog Prince & Princess Clock project) and others have dry-brushed finishing touches.

To produce a dry-brush effect, you must consider a number of factors, the first of which is the brush. There are hundreds to choose from; each artist has a favorite. Generally speaking, I recommend using the largest size that is comfortable to control for the given area to be painted. I prefer to use synthetic fibers for their spring or bounce.

Once a brush is chosen, the choice of medium and brush loading are next. The mediums I prefer for this technique are Jo Sonja's Clear Glazing Medium and Kleister Medium, for they add open time and translucency to the pigments when desired. Otherwise, I use the pigments at full strength.

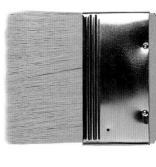

PAINTS

MISCELLANEOUS
SUPPLIES

MEDIUMS

Tee-Hee Tip

Although all projects name my
brand preferences for materials,
these brands are not required to
complete the projects. Use the
brands you prefer.

BRUSHES

7

TECHNIQUES, *continued*

Begin the brush loading with a clean, dry brush, dressed with the medium of choice. Next, fully load the brush to the ferrule with pigment (yes, this is a lot of paint in the brush!). However, before applying the paint to the design surface, take a moment to unload the tip or end of the bristles with a light stroke or two on the dry palette. This step removes excess paint, which makes it easier to achieve the broken-color application. The fully-loaded brush will carry the paint for a longer distance. The preceding steps seem to surprise most students, whether experienced or just learning the dry-brush technique. Those same students have had relative success with this method of brush loading, however. As with most things, success comes with patience, practice and perseverance.

Glazing

A glaze is a transparent or translucent pigment thinned with a medium, such as glaze, Kleister or water. I prefer Jo Sonja's Clear Glazing Medium. Mix the medium to a consistency needed to achieve the desired effects, such as texture and translucency.

The glazing technique is quite useful for creating a variety of effects. Multiple layers of pigment, wet-on-dry, achieve pigment strength in hue, value and chroma, thus adding to the depth of the painting.

I have used the glazing technique in two basic ways. One is the additive, or positive, technique of building a wet layer on a dry surface. Another glazing technique is known as the subtractive, or negative, in which the glaze is applied and then removed with a brush or tool. I have employed this technique using color plus Jo Sonja's Kleister Medium as the glaze and removing the design with a water-dampened brush (refer to the Pumpkin Carver project).

Wet-on-Wet

The wet-on-wet painting technique allows the artist to produce a blended gradation of hue, value and chroma with one or more pigments with the aid of a medium, in this case a retarder medium, which extends the drying time of the pigment.

Use this technique to diffuse edges or areas of the design (refer to the Pumpkin Carver and Santa & the Woodland Elves projects).

COLOR

I approach color partly by intuition and partly by technical knowledge. The emotional meaning of color expresses what is in my heart, a very important part of the creative process for every artist.

Being able to express the emotions felt in each design requires a balance of organizational techniques in order to achieve visual unity.

I follow the fundamental concepts of color based upon the Munsell system.

Here is the order of color families and the way I put them out on my wet palette. I use several layers of a quality paper towel, dampened with water and set flat into a shallow covered container.

The color families begin with the lightest values and go to the darkest values. They are squeezed out in a ½-inch (12 mm) puddle, side by side. (They may touch each other—after all, they are family!)

I find that the pigments stay wet longer without a lot of space between them which keeps the airflow at a minimum.

Prevent fast drying of your color palette by checking the moistness of the paper towels and watering them occasionally. Just lift a corner of the towel and pour cool water under the paper, allowing the water to percolate up through the towel and paints. Cover when not in use. I'm able to use a single palette for several months for those prolonged projects. No need to waste good paint!

COLOR CHART PAINTS=Jo Sonja's Artist's Colors

Titanium White

Smoked Pearl

Nimbus Grey

Raw Sienna

Provincial Beige

Brown Earth

Raw Umber

Carbon Black

Pale Gold Metallic

Sky Blue

Deep Plum

Dolphin Blue

Galaxy Blue

Charcoal

Yellow Light

Indian Yellow

Yellow Oxide

Jaune Brillant

Vermilion

Norwegian Orange

Rose Pink

Napthol Red Light

Burgundy

Purple Madder

Amethyst

Brilliant Violet

Dioxazine Purple

Moss Green

Brilliant Green

Pine Green

Celadon

Antique Green

Teal Green

Aqua

Ultramarine

Sapphire

Pacific Blue

Ultramarine Blue Deep

Pthalo Blue

The Ole' Fishin' Hole

Thoughts of the lazy, hazy days of summer conjure up sun-washed skies, surrounding hills and the ole' fishin' hole in my town. Somewhere, hidden in that pond, is this very special "hole" for local critters—faeries, frogs, flying fish—basking and bathing in the cool, calm water. Ahh…life is good!

I've chosen to work this design over a light-value background. This will help to do several things in our painting. First, it creates an illumination in the painting. It will make the transparent hues appear brighter. The light values will also allow us to use smaller amounts of dark values to create more contrast, especially in tiny areas. It also makes it easy for us to create a soft look using very little pigment and more translucent mediums.

The painting technique begins with brush sketching the design with an earth color that, when diluted with a medium, helps blend the design to the background.

A very important point to keep in mind as you build your painting is the relationship of the painting to the background. Everything comes from the background and goes back to it.

Another technique incorporated in this piece is a glazing technique. This is a process of laying thin, transparent pigment and a medium, wet-on-dry. It is a gradual building of hues. Let's enjoy this process, layer by layer!

The final detail strokes of lightest values help repeat the values of the background and thus soften the entire painting.

Pattern and Materials

This pattern may be hand-traced or photocopied for personal use only. Enlarge first at 200%, then at 143% to bring it to full size.

Jo Sonja's Artist's Gouache

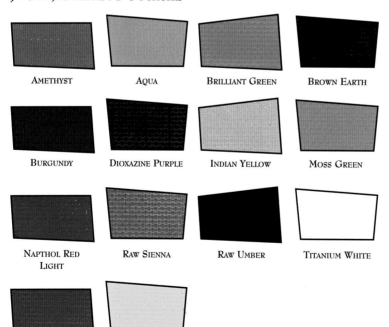

| AMETHYST | AQUA | BRILLIANT GREEN | BROWN EARTH |

| BURGUNDY | DIOXAZINE PURPLE | INDIAN YELLOW | MOSS GREEN |

| NAPTHOL RED LIGHT | RAW SIENNA | RAW UMBER | TITANIUM WHITE |

| ULTRAMARINE BLUE | YELLOW LIGHT |

Surface
- twig stool by Country Pleasures

Royal & Langnickel Aqualon Brushes
- no. 10/0 liner
- nos. 2, 3, 4 round
- nos. 6, 8, 10 filbert
- ½-inch (12mm) filbert

Additional Supplies
- cloth
- gray graphite paper
- Jo Sonja's Clear Glazing Medium
- Jo Sonja's Kleister Medium
- Jo Sonja's Satin Varnish
- J.W. etc. White Lightning
- medium-grit sandpaper
- stylus

Preparing the Surface and Brush Sketching

RAW SURFACE ▲

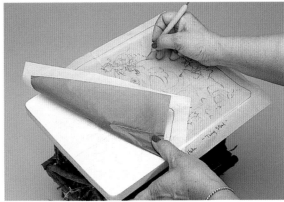

1 Apply two thin coats of White Lightning, drying between coats. Sand the surface lightly with a medium-grit sandpaper. Wipe with a dry cloth. Use gray graphite paper and a stylus to transfer the pattern.

Tee-Hee Tip

Using the pattern is optional. If you prefer, throw away your pattern and just go for it!

2 In an impressionistic style (loose, short, choppy strokes), begin brush sketching using a round brush loaded with Raw Sienna and Kleister Medium (1:1 brush mixed). The size of the round brush depends on you. If you're heavy-handed, use a smaller brush. I use a no. 4 in this step. Your brush pressure will determine the stroke width.

Tee-Hee Tip

You can use Kleister Medium to help erase your graphite lines.

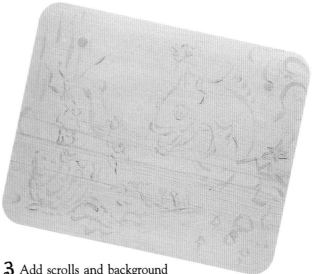

3 Add scrolls and background elements, such as the reeds. Remember to add your personality into the sketching.

Brush Sketching, *continued*

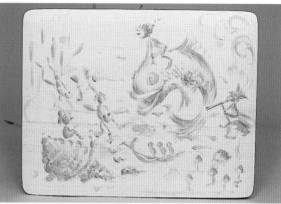

4 With a no. 6 or 8 filbert, add Kleister Medium + Brown Earth to develop form and shadows. Use short sketchy strokes to create soft edges. Where you want more paint, apply more pressure. Overlap the edges for a soft appearance. Go about three-quarters of the way across as shown.

5 Paint the items in the water and in the foreground, and work back into the background. Leave the background impressionistic. This leaves room for the viewer's imagination. Start with the center of interest, checking back to that point often. Feel free to smudge the paint with your fingers.

6 Using the dirty brush, side-load into Raw Umber. Come about halfway into the previous color. Work to deepen the shadows and create the illusion of roundness to the curved shapes with middle to dark values.

7 Evaluate your painting at this point. Hold it at arm's length and squint. Make sure your light-to-dark value changes are well executed.

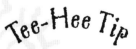

Tee-Hee Tip

Don't try to get too refined with your painting. Use a larger brush and broader strokes in the beginning.

8 Mix Raw Umber + Dioxazine Purple on your dirty brush. Start at the center of interest and dab shapes with Cs and Vs. Plop in an eyeball. Begin to add a little more detail, but remember, you're still in the sketching-in stage. Move color throughout your painting to create flow and rhythm.

9 Drybrush and slip-slap with a flat brush. Add touches of Raw Sienna + Kleister Medium to the sides and top. Apply a thinned mix of Raw Sienna + Brown Earth + Raw Umber + Dioxazine Purple to the edges and corners of your piece. Keep in mind where it would be worn with age. Put the darker colors in the corners to create this antiquing effect.

10 Eliminating the light background draws the viewer to the center of interest, which, in this case, is the fish. The values are directional finders. They tell the viewer where to look. The detail in the background for this piece is very Impressionistic and blurry, so it doesn't draw the eye. Side-load a filbert brush with Dioxazine Purple + Kleister Medium. You don't want this color to be too strong. Dab reflections under the boat, giving it a sense of water. Carry this color throughout the design. Use less paint as you fade into the background. This creates the illusion of distance.

11 The dark values of the snails and mushrooms hold them down on the ground. Side-load Raw Umber + Dioxazine Purple, and dab into the shadow areas. Don't forget to step back and take a look at your piece to make sure the values are strong enough.

Tee-Hee Tip

When you want to soften edges or push an element into the background, take the object closer to the background value, hue and intensity. It then becomes more like the background!

Glazing

12 A glaze is a thin or transparent pigment. The technique of glazing is a layering of transparent pigment, wet-on-dry. (See page 8.) Apply multiple layers to build the strength of pigment. You can use any medium to thin your paint, but be consistent throughout your piece. Start with the warmest and lightest colors on your palette. Progress from yellow to red to green to blue to violet. Add sunshine,mostly to the center of interest. The cooler colors go in the shadows and around the perimeter of the piece. Work with a clean brush for the fullest strength of color and dance this color around the painting to carry color throughout. Next go from the Yellow Light to Indian Yellow. Now you need to stay out of the highlight area, but don't forget to dance this color around the rest of the piece, in weaker and smaller amounts. Add more glazing medium to weaken the pigment.

13 Side-load a no. 10 filbert with Napthol Red Light thinned with the glaze medium. The side load of pigment helps to control the strongest amount of color. Stay out of the highlight areas, but walk the color toward the highlight, keeping in mind the texture of the element. Glaze the colors wet-on-dry.

14 Add accents to bugs and mushrooms throughout the design. Glaze the mushrooms on the shadow side. Control the strength of the color with the medium. Here I used Burgundy.

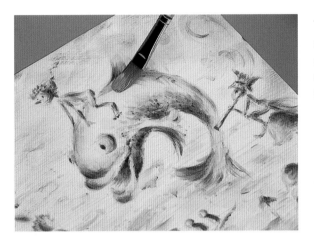

15 Add Brilliant Green to some of the light value areas. Mix the green with Clear Glazing Medium to control the strength. Start at the center of interest and work your way out. Don't forget to dab the color throughout your design.

16 Use Aqua + Kleister Medium on a small filbert to create scales on the fish. Move throughout your painting, staying out of the highlight areas. Add mostly to the green areas, starting at the center of interest and moving outward as there is less paint on your brush.

17 Remember to move the Aqua around the painting.

Developing Details

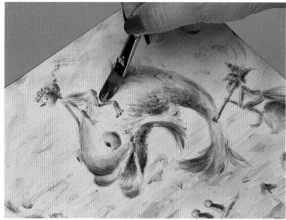

18 Side-load Ultramarine Blue on the wiped, dirty brush. Apply more of this color to the shadow areas. Strengthen the darker areas by dabbing.

19 Be sure to move the Ultramarine Blue around the painting, keeping it in the shadow areas. Cool the Burgundy on the mushrooms and the shadows on the snail. Apply to the water area with streaks. Vary the strength and size of the dabs.

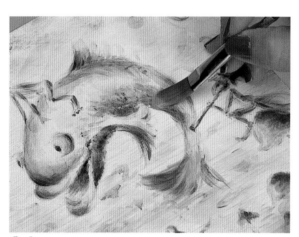

20 Apply Amethyst into darker areas. This produces a wispy veil of color. For a stronger violet hue, use Dioxazine Purple.

21 Amethyst creates a hazy look. To create this effect, hold way back on the brush handle and swirl in the sky and water.

22 With a ½-inch (12mm) filbert brush loaded with Moss Green thinned with Kleister Medium, basecoat the water lilies. Clean the brush.

23 Side-load Ultramarine Blue on the filbert brush. Shade the underside of the lilypads, starting in the foreground of the design. As there is less and less paint on the brush, move to the background. Let the brush wiggle so there aren't any definite edges.

24 Apply the split of the water lily using a clean ½-inch (12mm) filbert brush side-loaded with Ultramarine Blue.

25 Load a ½-inch (12mm) filbert with Moss Green + a touch of Titanium White (brush mixed), and apply next to the shadow area on the water lilies to create more contrast. Repeat as needed.

Developing Details, *continued*

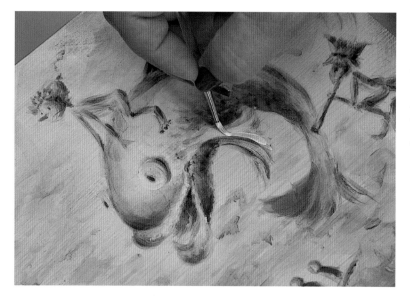

26 With a no. 2 round brush, highlight the front of the fish eye with Titanium White + a touch of Yellow Light and Clear Glazing Medium. Also, add the transparent white on the lip and dab on the back of the fish to simulate water drops. Add the fins to the fish to increase the luminosity.

27 Stipple the edges of the hats with Titanium White + Clear Glazing Medium. Add Yellow Light + Titanium White to the front of the faeries' faces with a small round or liner brush.

28 Add more detailing to the faeries, under the mushrooms, in the water and on the snail with Titanium White and a touch of Yellow Light. These added sparks of warm, light dots add a touch of magic to the painting.

Faerie on Frog

29 With a small round brush, brush sketch your design with Raw Sienna mixed with Kleister Medium. Next, shade with the same mix. Then apply Brown Earth, and finally, add Raw Umber.

Snail

3 Load a small round brush with Raw Sienna + Kleister Medium and brush sketch the design, except the wings. With a no. 6 filbert, paint the first dark value, Raw Sienna + Kleister Medium, from back to front of the faerie and snail bodies, to create some dimensional shapes. Load Brown Earth + Kleister Medium in the dirty brush.

Place this color within the previous color, blending or fading out before reaching the outer edges or lighter-value areas. This dark value strengthens and reinforces the shapes. Next, load Raw Umber + Kleister Medium onto your brush. This gives the shapes added punch. The darker value creates more contrast against the light background and brings it into view and better form.

Ladybugs on Boat & Lilypads

31 For both the ladybugs on boat and the lilypads, brush sketch Raw Sienna + Kleister Medium with a small, round brush. Add more Raw Sienna + Kleister Medium. Next, add Brown Earth and then Raw Umber.

Praying Mantis & Mushrooms

32 Brush sketch the praying mantis with Raw Sienna. Shade with Raw Sienna to create form. Shade again with Raw Sienna + Brown Earth.

Next shading is with Brown Earth + Raw Umber.

Shade again with Raw Umber + Dioxazine Purple.

For the mushroom, follow the praying mantis steps and then apply flesh mix: Titanium White + Yellow Light + Napthol Red Light.

33 Apply a Brilliant Green glaze to the body. Stroke a Napthol Red Light glaze on the headdress. Apply a glaze of Burgundy over the Napthol Red Light. Add a few Amethyst strokes to the headdress and the darkest areas of the body.

Apply a glaze of Titanium White and Yellow Light on the headdress, wings, body, eyes, face, horn, arms, and stripes on legs. The eye dot is Dioxazine Purple. Cross-hatch a few detail lines to accentuate features of the eyelids, mouth and wings.

Next, glaze the mushroom with Napthol Red Light.

After that, add Burgundy to the dark value overlapping Napthol Red Light. Add a touch of Amethyst to the darkest areas. Dab a few dots of Titanium White + Raw Sienna with a no. 3 round brush.

Casually add final details with a lighter-value mix of Titanium White + a touch of Yellow Light to dots, lacy edge along the bottom of the mushroom cap, collar and stem.

Faerie, Snail & Ladybugs on Boat

34 The fourth dark shading consists of loading Dioxazine Purple + Kleister Medium on a dirty, small round brush. This gives the added core dark color needed to complete the forms. Look at the darkest values, and add just a touch of this darkest mix where needed.

35 The first glazing step is with Yellow Light + Clear Glazing Medium. Begin application over light-value areas.

Faerie, Snail & Ladybugs on Boat, *continued*

36 Apply Indian Yellow onto midvalue areas, overlapping some of the lightest and darkest areas for gradation of hue. You may add a touch of Clear Glazing Medium to the pigment to allow for ease of movement.

The flesh areas are Titanium White + Yellow Light + Napthol Red Light.

37 Now, glaze Napthol Red Light from the dark values out to the light values: cheeks, bottoms of noses, ladybugs' backs and touches on the canoe, frog and snail shell. The glaze is light on the cheeks and nose, and only a touch on arms and legs. You must overlap the darkest-value areas.

38 Highlight faces, arms and legs with a brush mix of Titanium White + a touch of Yellow Light. Highlights go on the fronts and tops of the facial and body parts. Glaze them with Brilliant Green.

Base the ladybug faces in Titanium White + a touch of Yellow Light.

For the water lilypads, follow the water lily step-by-step instructions on page 19 beginning with step 22. Glaze may be applied to the water lilypads later in the painting process. Final detail lines are a mix of Moss Green + Ultramarine Blue + water. Add highlights (Titanium White + a touch of Yellow Light) in dots and dashes.

39 With a no. 3 round loaded with a mix of Aqua + Titanium White + a touch of Clear Glazing Medium, stroke and dot this mix on the darker-value painted areas. This step does several things. It adds a temperature change for contrast, lightens the warm areas and softens the overall painting when overlapping the dark values and making the value closer to the light background.

Faerie, Snail & Ladybug Grouping, *continued*

40 Next add a few more details with a mix of Titanium White + a touch of Yellow Light on a no. 3 round brush, and then more white with the dirty brush. Paint one-stroke petals on the hats. Apply comma strokes to wings. Make **S**-strokes across the faeries' chests and legs to cover them. Paint a **C**-stroke on the snail shell.

With Brilliant Green + Clear Glazing Medium, stipple dots on frog body. Then stipple more dots with a mix of Titanium White + Yellow Light.

With Titanium White, use a large brush and dot the eye placement on the snail and the frog. Add streaky strokes onto the ladybugs' heads and bodies. Add a few touches to highlight the snail faerie's armhole and boat.

41 For the final glazes, use Amethyst + Dioxazine Purple over the darkest values as desired, for interest. For example, I have chosen to glaze the base of the flower petals and wings, water, rocks, snail and shell.

For the ladybug crew, now add the detail linework. The dark linework is a mix of Raw Umber + Dioxazine Purple. This includes hair, eyes, antennae, arms and dots. The light value linework is Titanium White on the arms and the oars.

42 Follow instructions for the faerie, snail & lady-bugs on boat when painting the fish.

Hoppin' Down the Bunny Trail

Here comes the Easter Bunny just in time for the Easter Parade—wearing his finest garb and carting decorated eggs for giving.

The painting techniques are the same as for the Birthday Party Bop and The Ole' Fishin' Hole projects. Enjoy the process!

Pattern

These patterns may be hand-traced or photocopied for personal use only.
Enlarge first at 200%, then at 125% to bring them to full size.

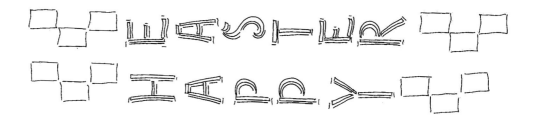

Materials

Jo Sonja's Artist's Gouache

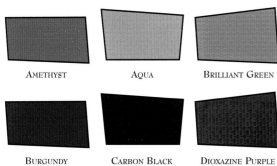

 AMETHYST

 **AQUA**

 BRILLIANT GREEN

 BROWN EARTH

BURGUNDY

CARBON BLACK

DIOXAZINE PURPLE

MOSS GREEN

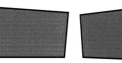 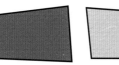

NAPTHOL RED LIGHT

PROVINCIAL BEIGE

RAW SIENNA

SMOKED PEARL

TITANIUM WHITE

ULTRAMARINE BLUE

VERMILION

YELLOW LIGHT

YELLOW OXIDE

Surface

- Bentwood tray

Royal & Langnickel Aqualon Brushes

- 10/0 liner
- ¾-inch (19mm) wash
- nos. 2 & 3 round
- no. 10 filbert
- no. 12 shader

Additional Supplies

- cloth
- gray graphite paper
- Jo Sonja's Clear Glazing Medium
- Jo Sonja's Kleister Medium
- Jo Sonja's Satin Varnish
- J.W. etc. White Lightning
- medium- to fine-grit sandpaper
- stylus

RAW SURFACE ▶

33

Brush Sketching

1 Apply two coats of White Lightning over the entire box with a large flat brush. Allow to dry between coats. Lightly sand with a medium- to fine-grit sandpaper. Wipe with a dry, lint-free cloth. Transfer the pattern using your stylus and gray graphite paper.

Brush sketch with Raw Sienna, especially in the shading areas.

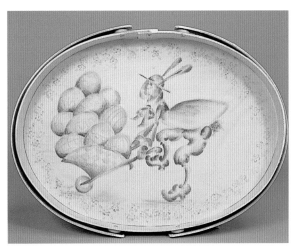

2 Brush sketch with the second shading color, Brown Earth.

3 Brush sketch with the final shading color, Brown Earth + Dioxazine Purple. As you get darker, the shading goes in a smaller area.

Applying the Glazes

4 Glaze the highlight or warm areas with Yellow Light. Use the background for the lightest light. It is important to incorporate the background into the entire painting and border area. Add interest and depth to the background and border with the Yellow Light glaze applied randomly.

5 Apply the base colors: Vermilion on the pants and eggs; Brilliant Green to the bow tie and eggs; Amethyst to the coat, eggs and background. On the hands, face and legs, apply Provincial Beige. Apply Brown Earth and Brilliant Green checks on the wheelbarrow and a wash of Carbon Black on the hat.

6 Apply Amethyst + a touch of Brown Earth as an antiquing medium along the perimeter.

7 Strengthen the shadows by layering on more of the base color or a darker member of that color family.

8 Strengthen the highlights with warmer and lighter colors.

9 Base in the green spots on the jacket with Brilliant Green.

Applying the Glazes, *continued*

10 Add the linework on the legs, head, hands, teeth and eggs using a 10/0 liner brush loaded with Brown Earth.

11 Darken the detailing using the 10/0 liner brush loaded with Carbon Black. Go over the previous linework.

RABBIT
DETAIL

Rabbit Head and Glasses

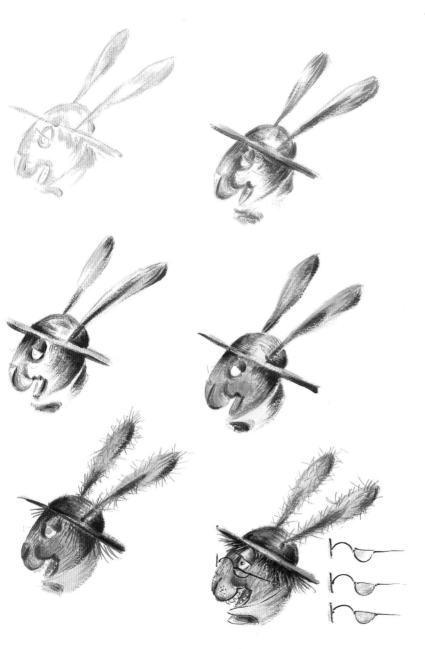

12 Brush sketch the rabbit head using a no. 3 round loaded with Raw Sienna + Kleister Medium. Now, strengthen the shaded areas with Brown Earth + Kleister Medium. Stroke the brush from the darkest areas out to the midvalue areas. Add more dark value into the V- and C-shaded areas with a mix of Brown Earth + Dioxazine Purple with a touch of Kleister Medium.

Next, add translucent base colors to all areas with a brush mix of Kleister Medium + your preferred color. For the body, use Provincial Beige. For the nose, cheek, ear, and inside of mouth, use Vermilion + glaze. Base the eye in Titanium White.

Next, strengthen the base colors with darker family values or another layer of the basecoat color. For the eye, use Aqua; for the hair, use Brown Earth; for the collar and teeth, use Smoked Pearl.

Finally on the rabbit head, apply lighter values as desired in order to achieve more contrast and detail. Lighten the hair, eye and teeth with a touch of Titanium White and detail with a black liner. Make whisker dots with the black liner.

For the glasses, use the black liner to outline the frame. Use Aqua + Titanium White (1:1) for the upper left of the lens. Apply Amethyst + Titanium White (1:1) for the lower right part of the lens. Highlight the lens with a streak of Yellow Light + Titanium White across the center of the glass.

Letters and Flowers

13 Brush sketch the letters onto the tray handles with Raw Sienna. Load a no. 2 round with Brown Earth + a touch of Dioxazine Purple + a touch of water and shadow the left side and bottom of each letter. Then accent the lettering with tints (color + Titanium White + Kleister Medium) of Yellow Light, Vermilion, Brilliant Green, Aqua and Amethyst.

For the flower border, first paint the background with Moss Green/ Vermilion/Amethyst + Smoked Pearl + Kleister Medium. Use a no. 3 round loaded with Raw Sienna and brush sketch. Next, apply Aqua + Titanium White + Kleister. Then, add Amethyst + Titanium White + Kleister Medium. Paint the leaves with Moss Green + a touch of Brilliant Green + Kleister Medium.

Paint the stripes with a ¾-inch (19mm) wash brush loaded with Yellow Oxide + Smoked Pearl + Kleister Medium.

To antique, use a ¾-inch (19mm) wash brush and slip-slap Brown Earth + Amethyst + Kleister Medium or Brown Earth + Dioxazine Purple + Kleister Medium.

Finally, do linework with a 10/0 liner and Carbon Black + water.

Completed Tray

TOP VIEW

SIDE VIEW

The Faerie Garden

The Faerie Garden idea came to mind one day as thoughts went back to Grandma and Mom lovingly tending their gardens, and sharing plants and cuttings with friends and neighbors. My mother believed that her daily chats kept the plants happy and healthy because they felt loved. Works for people, too!

The techniques for this painting are varied. The key factor to remember as we go through the process of each stage is *soft*. Creating a soft effect is easier than you may think. Begin with hues that are closest to the value, hue and intensity of the background. This is a very important step. In any art medium we choose, the relationship of the background to the painting is key. The use of Kleister Medium, which is a semitransparent medium, helps greatly to control the strength of the pigment.

Work with a "dirty brush" (paint left from previous application and blended with the succeeding pigments). Wipe the brush on a dry towel to remove excess pigment if needed.

A gradual layering and overlapping of edges creates softness. Play back and forth, develop stronger contrasts and then step back to observe and evaluate.

Practice and experimentation are great teachers. Never give up…it's just paint!

Pattern

This pattern may be hand-traced or photocopied for personal use only. Join the patterns at the dashed lines. Enlarge at 125% to bring it to full size.

Materials

Jo Sonja's Artist's Gouache

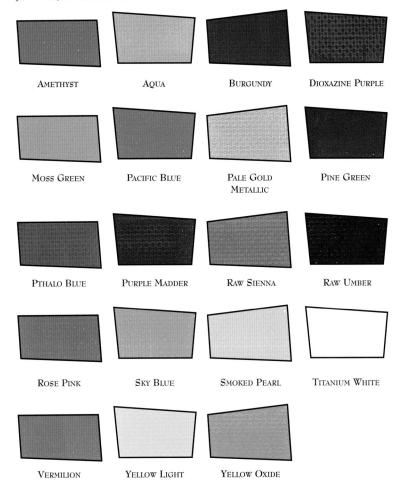

Amethyst	Aqua	Burgundy	Dioxazine Purple
Moss Green	Pacific Blue	Pale Gold Metallic	Pine Green
Pthalo Blue	Purple Madder	Raw Sienna	Raw Umber
Rose Pink	Sky Blue	Smoked Pearl	Titanium White
Vermilion	Yellow Light	Yellow Oxide	

Surface

- round wooden birdhouse by Country Pleasures

Royal & Langnickel Aqualon Brushes

- no. 6 filbert
- no. 10/0 liner
- nos. 2, 3 round
- ¾-inch (19mm) wash

Royal & Langnickel Royal Sable Brushes

- no. 8 duster
- no. 6 short round

Additional Supplies

- gray graphite paper
- Jo Sonja's Clear Glazing Medium
- Jo Sonja's Kleister Medium
- J.W. etc. matte varnish
- stylus

Preparing the Surface

RAW SURFACE ▲

1 Basecoat the birdhouse with Sky Blue. Transfer the pattern using gray graphite paper and a stylus.

Background

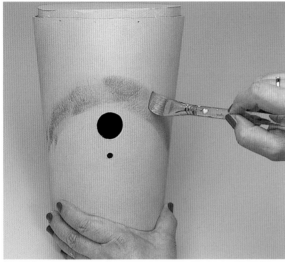

2 Start with the color closest to the background. To create the effect of early morning, work wet-on-wet using a ¾-inch (19mm) glaze brush loaded with Kleister Medium and Pacific Blue. The bristles should barely touch the surface. This light touch creates a broken, soft effect.

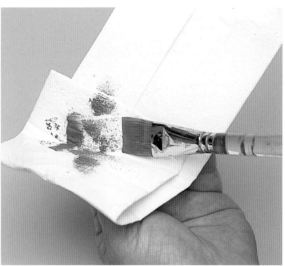

3 Just wipe the brush—don't rinse it!—because we are dirty brush blending. This leaves the previous color in the brush to "marry" with the next.

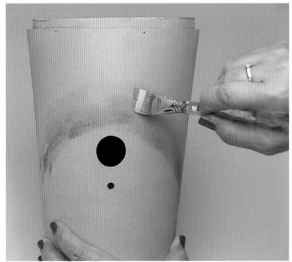

4 Using the wiped ¾-inch (19mm) glaze brush loaded with Kleister Medium + Amethyst + a touch of Titanium White, slightly overlap the previous color walking it in and out to get a soft blend of the colors. Dry wipe the brush.

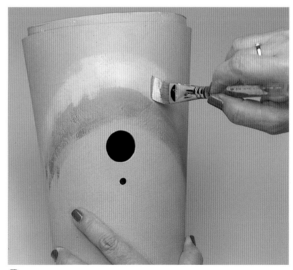

5 Pick up Yellow Oxide + a touch of Titanium White on the brush. Stroke across the top and let the color disappear on the sides. Again, work it back and forth into the previous color. Wipe the brush.

Background, *continued*

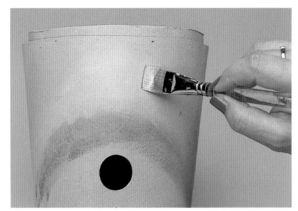

6 Pick up Vermilion + a touch of Titanium White + Kleister Medium on the wiped brush. Drybrush at the top of the arc.

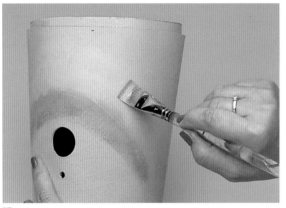

7 Blend it into the previous color and off to one side.

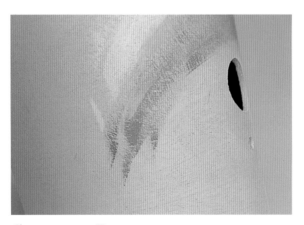

COMPLETED RAINBOW

OOPS! DID THIS HAPPEN TO YOU?

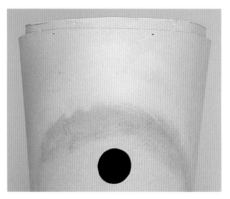

There is too much contrast. The blue is too dark.

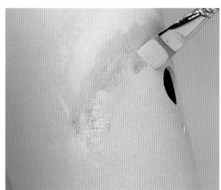

When you want less contrast in the background, go back and use the background color plus a touch of Kleister Medium to soften the color. Drybrush this mix into the background and the rainbow to lose the hard edges.

Flowers and Foliage

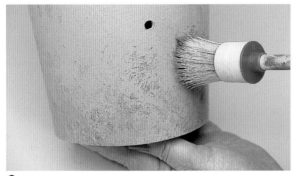

8 Using a no. 8 duster brush loaded with Kleister Medium + Pine Green, stipple in the background grasses. Turn and twist the brush so you get a variety of patterns.

9 Mix in a little Raw Umber with the Pine Green and Kleister Medium to create a darker green and more value and tonal contrast. Apply this mix to the bottom of the piece. Keep the brush as dry as possible, and use only the tip of the brush. Dry wipe the brush.

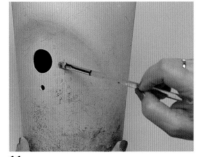

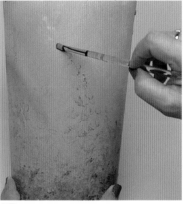

10 With a tint of Moss Green + Smoked Pearl (1:1) on the duster brush, break up the background with swirls and graceful curves. Be sure to come off the edge. Apply this to the top of the birdhouse. This step creates movement, depth and interest.

11 Apply the foxglove and hollyhock leaves with a no. 6 filbert brush and a lot of Kleister Medium + a touch of Pine Green for a translucent color. Hold the brush near the handle's end. Start at the bottom edge of the grass with ghostly plops. The overall shape is an elongated triangle.

12 Continue with the ghostly plops and taper to the top. As you get to the top, you should use the least amount of pressure for a gradation of large to small sizes.

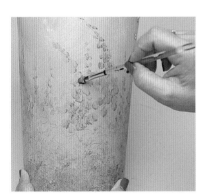

13 Tone the leaves with a mix of Raw Umber + Pine Green + Kleister Medium to keep the mix thin. Apply these toned leaves about halfway up, on and off the edges, overlapping other leaf shapes.

Foxgloves & Hollyhocks

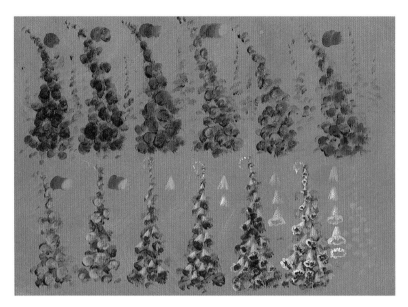

14 For the red hollyhocks, load a no. 6 filbert with Dioxazine Purple + Kleister Medium (6:1). Base the flowers with squishy dabs. Place the flowers randomly, starting with large flowers at the bottom and small ones at the top.

Add a mix of Burgundy + Kleister Medium (1:6) on top. Again, place this layer randomly over the first step.

Next, apply Rose Pink + a touch of Smoked Pearl thinned with Kleister Medium. Wiggle the brush slightly.

With your dirty brush, apply Kleister Medium + a touch of Vermilion for translucency.

Stipple Vermilion + Yellow Light + Titanium White (1:1:1) with the tip of a 10/0 liner for the center detail.

15 Base the blue hollyhocks with a no. 6 filbert loaded with Pacific Blue + Kleister Medium. Base flowers, using random placement as before.

Add a mix of Burgundy + Kleister Medium (1:6) on top.

Add Aqua + a touch of Smoked Pearl + Kleister Medium.

Strengthen the light value on a few edges with a mix of Aqua + a touch of Titanium White + a touch of Yellow Light. Stipple Vermilion + Yellow Light + Titanium White (1:1:1) with the tip of a 10/0 liner for the center dots.

16 With a no. 6 filbert loaded with Dioxazine Purple + Kleister Medium (6:1), base the foxgloves with squishy dabs. Place the flowers randomly, starting with large flowers at the top and small at the bottom.

Now, shape the foxgloves into triangles with Smoked Pearl + Kleister Medium. Do this linework with a small round or a larger liner brush. The stem ends point toward the imaginary center stem.

Develop the height of the triangle shapes with the liner strokes. Begin your stroke near the middle of a triangle and walk the paint out to the edge, very softly.

Add a ruffled edge with Smoked Pearl + Kleister Medium using a 10/0 liner.

Add Titanium White to the liner and wiggle this light value on the top of the ruffled opening.

Add a few dabs of Vermilion + Yellow Light + Titanium White (1:1:1) to the flower center.

Add a final touch of dabbled leaves with a mix of Kleister Medium + Moss Green + Smoked Pearl (1:1:1). This will add a spark of light to the leafy areas. This step softens the overall effect.

Frogs

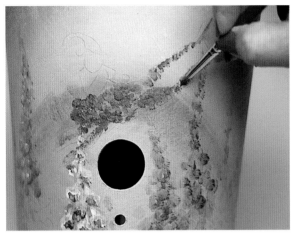

17 Base in the shape of the frog by stippling with a no. 6 round loaded with Pine Green + Kleister Medium + Raw Umber.

18 Stipple the frog in the flowers just as you did the previous frog. Wipe the brush.

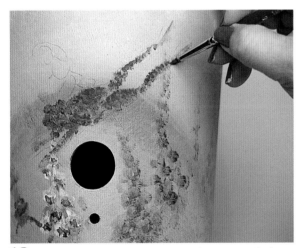

19 Stipple Purple Madder from the top and about halfway down using the no. 6 round. Stipple as you did the previous color. Paint right over the faerie.

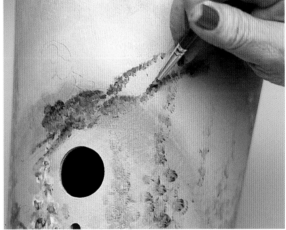

20 Using the dirty brush loaded with Dioxazine Purple + Kleister Medium, create more shading on the top part of the frog. Then apply Pine Green + Aqua + Kleister Medium in the same stippling motion going in and out of the darker values from the lower edge of the frog's body to the middle areas.

Frogs, *continued*

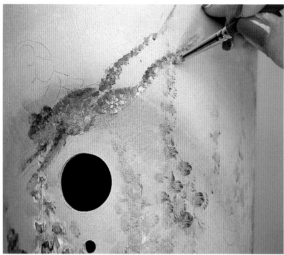

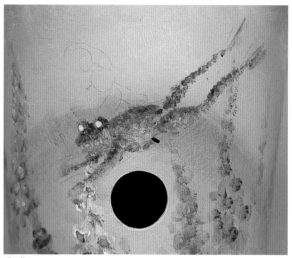

21 Add Aqua + Pale Gold Metallic + Kleister Medium on the tip of the brush, and stipple on the belly and lower area of the frog. You can add a touch of Titanium White to the above mix to create a super highlight if you wish.

22 Mix Titanium White + Yellow Light (10:1) to create the eyeballs. Tap them in so they look like headlights.

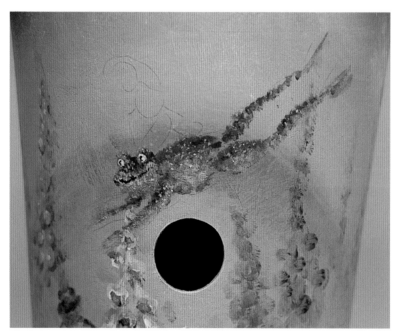

23 Mix Dioxazine Purple + Pine Green for the pupils and mouth. Create a wobbly line for the mouth, nostrils and lips. Wipe the brush. Mix Moss Green + Titanium White (1:2) and paint the lips, cheeks and the light-value dots on the frog's body. This makes the frog look wet. Add more contrast with Yellow Light + Titanium White (1:4). Glaze the cheeks with any of the reds.

Faeries

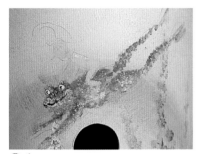  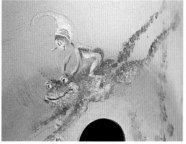

24 Mix Vermilion + a touch of Titanium White to create the flesh color. Evaluate this color against the background. Add a little more Vermilion to the mix if necessary. Wipe the brush.

25 Take the Vermilion mix + Dioxazine Purple and shade the back of the body with a no. 2 round brush. Wipe the brush.

26 Highlight the front of the body with Yellow Light + Titanium White + Kleister Medium. You'll get a stronger color at first. Use short, choppy strokes. Mix Kleister Medium + Titanium White in an overloaded stroke to make the hat.

27 For the clothes and wings, use a no. 3 round heavily loaded with Kleister Medium + Titanium White. Apply with wavy strokes. Vary the stroke with more pressure on the brush for more width, and then lift gradually to the brush tip to finish the stroke.

Pansies

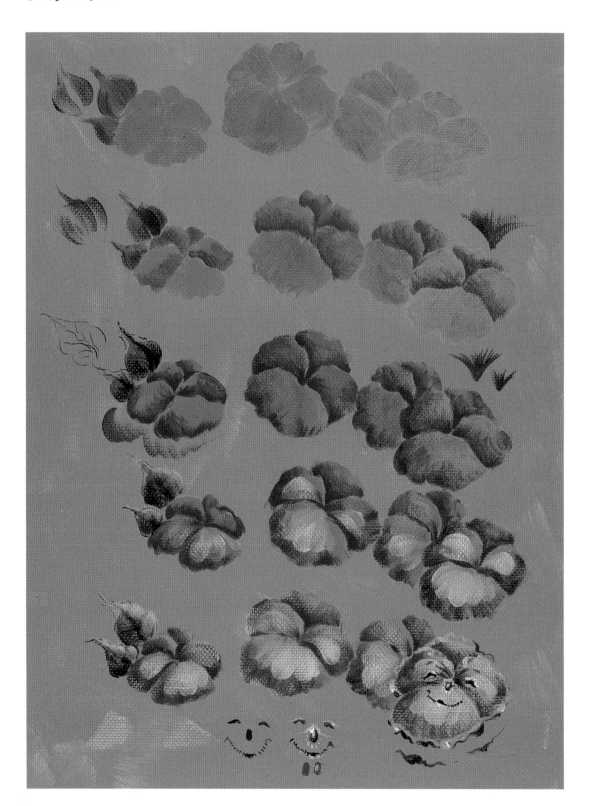

28 Base the different pansies with a lot of Kleister Medium + pigment: Pthalo Blue, Amethyst, Raw Sienna or Rose Pink. Base the front, side and back petals with the translucent colors. These will appear as very vague shapes without definition. Allow the background to separate the petals.

Paint the filler leaves with a filbert or round brush. These are two-stroke leaves starting at the tip and going to the stem end. Use Pine Green + Kleister + a touch of Raw Umber.

Make linear leaves with a press, pull, wiggle stroke. Let this dry. Be sure to keep low contrast on the leaves. This keeps the leaves in the background.

29 On a few leaves, highlight the stroke with Kleister Medium + Moss Green.

For all the pansies, use a filbert brush side-loaded with the base color + Purple Madder + Kleister. Separate the front petals from the back and side petals, walking the Purple Madder from the darkest point and fading it into the middle value.

30 Now you can decide where you want a petal to roll. Where it is going to roll, apply the dark value.

Mix Kleister Medium + Smoked Pearl so you can see through it. Test it on your hand to see if it's transparent. Press down on the outer edge of your petal. Pull into the center and lift to fill in the eye patch. The Smoked Pearl will begin to disappear as it dries.

31 Highlight the pansies using a filbert brush with the base color of the pansy plus Titanium White to create a tint. Stroke from the outside into the center. Drybrush it if you need more texture. If you need further highlights, mix Titanium White + Smoked Pearl.

Add accent colors by mixing Titanium White with the different family colors. Start with the yellows and work your way through the other color families. Create more punch with a contrasting color in hue, temperature or intensity. Apply it lightly and softly.

Put Light Yellow in the highlight areas for a lift in the dark-value areas—as a discord. Dance color throughout the piece.

32 For the facial features, use a no. 10/0 liner or a small round brush to sketch the eyes, nose and mouth in Purple Madder. Dance a few squiggles along the pansies' petals to create a cast shadow effect. Brighten the nose with a dab of Vermilion, then Yellow Light + Titanium White. Touch this to the lower lip.

Jiggle a very lacy edge of Titanium White + Kleister Medium with the liner or the round along the petals, eyelids, nose bridge and mustache.

Final Touches

33 Using a round brush loaded with Kleister Medium + Titanium White, add lacy-looking ruffles around the edges of the pansy petals.

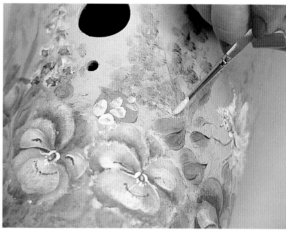

34 Paint the filler ferns with a no. 3 round brush loaded with Moss Green + Titanium White (1:1) and plenty of Kleister Medium for translucent, textured dabs of paint.

35 Use the dry-brush technique to add more texture to the background. Load the duster brush with Moss Green + Smoked Pearl (1:1) + Kleister Medium and really work it into the brush. Pounce on the palette.

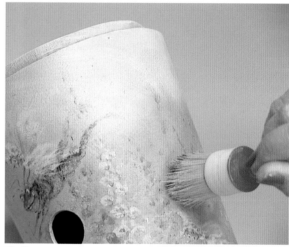

36 Make wispy dry-brush C-strokes starting at the edge of the piece, landing and lifting off the surface. See page 6 for detailed instructions about drybrushing.

37 The letters are linear strokes of Purple Madder. Add highlight strokes of Pale Gold Metallic to the tops and fronts of each letter. Drybrush a final dusting of Pale Gold Metallic + a touch of Kleister Medium with a ¾-inch (19mm) glaze brush over the finial and birdhouse. Dry. Apply a coat of varnish.

Enjoy your fantasy garden!

4

Birthday Party Box

This is a birthday box for you. Some very whimsical creatures are helping to celebrate your day. These enchanting party pals are from my imagination. The inspiration comes from my love of nature and God's little creatures.

The technique is the same as used for The Ole' Fishin' Hole project: brush sketching and glazing. Soft swirls of color throughout, especially in the background and perimeter, create an airy, fuzzy-edged painting. Sharper details are on the front and center objects in very small amounts. The White Lightning sealer and basecoat help to illuminate the picture with happy, bright colors which are just right for this happy, festive occasion.

Pattern

These patterns may be hand-traced or photocopied for personal use only. Enlarge the lettering pattern first at 200%, then at 111% and the middle pattern at 182% to bring them to full size.

Enlarge the patterns below at 143% to bring them to full size.

Materials

Jo Sonja's Artist's Gouache

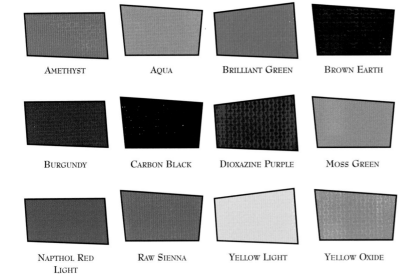

Amethyst	Aqua	Brilliant Green	Brown Earth
Burgundy	Carbon Black	Dioxazine Purple	Moss Green
Napthol Red Light	Raw Sienna	Yellow Light	Yellow Oxide

Surface

◎ wood box by Country Pleasures

Royal & Langnickel Aqualon Brushes

◎ no. 3 round
◎ ¾-inch (19mm) wash

Additional Supplies

◎ cloth
◎ gray graphite paper
◎ Jo Sonja's Kleister Medium
◎ Jo Sonja's Clear Glazing Medium
◎ J.W. etc. White Lightning
◎ medium-grit sandpaper
◎ stylus

Tee-Hee Tip

Seal your surfaces with no more than two coats of White Lightning. Otherwise, the surface may become too slick.

RAW SURFACE ▶

Brush Sketching

1 Use gray graphite paper and a stylus to transfer the pattern. Brush sketch your design with Raw Sienna + Kleister Medium using a no. 3 round brush.

2 Brush sketch with the same brush loaded with Brown Earth.

3 Brush sketch the third layer with a mix of Brown Earth + a touch of Dioxazine Purple on the same brush.

Adding Color

4 Add Yellow Light + Clear Glazing Medium in the highlight areas using the largest, most comfortable brush available.

5 Mix Yellow Oxide + Clear Glazing Medium. Apply in the shaded areas, and stay out of the highlights. This is very subtle. The forms take shape gradually.

6 Lower the intensity around the perimeter of the piece with a warm color. Use Raw Sienna + Clear Glazing Medium on a side-loaded ¾-inch (19mm) wash brush.

7 Start in the shaded areas with the first red glaze, Napthol Red Light. Glaze things that are red, such as the mushroom caps and the ladybugs.

8 Now add the Brilliant Green glaze just as you did the previous glazes. Add the green to the frog's body, the turtle and the flies.

9 Add the Aqua glaze using the same technique. Add the Aqua to the caterpillar and to the chick's hat.

Adding Color, *continued*

10 Add the Amethyst glaze using the same brush. Use this color on the caterpillar's bottom section and over the dark-shaded areas of each object. Add a touch of Amethyst glaze to the background sky.

11 Add Carbon Black to the center of interest where you want to draw attention, and to the objects which are smallest in size: the ants, the eyes and the legs.

Chicken

Frog, Chick, Squirrel & Ladybug

Caterpillar, Flies & Lettering

Ants & Birthday Cake

Bottom

12 Basecoat the box bottom with White Lightning.

13 Wash Raw Sienna over the top section. Wipe the brush. Wash Moss Green thinned with Clear Glazing Medium over the third section. Wipe the brush. Apply a wash of thinned Burgundy over the entire piece. With a ¾-inch (19mm) flat brush, apply the checks to the bottom section.

Finished Box

SIDE VIEW ▶

▲ TOP VIEW

◀ Inside

Completed Box ▶

5

Jack Frost & the Snowflake Faeries

Jack Frost is winter's jester, changing the landscape from autumn's warm brilliant hues to a palette of frosty blues and grays. Jack is holding a bag of tricks that is filled with dancing snowflake faeries to add a touch of winter whimsy.

As I set out to create this magical winter setting, much like a Jack Frost, I decided to play a trick or two, playing with the palette. I decided to use a "clash" of hues to vibrate the viewer's eyes.

The techniques applied are a combination of illumination from the white undercoat and the translucent overcoat of reds. Overlapping design elements, values, hues and chroma adds the wow factor.

To one flake from another…

Tee Hee.

Pattern

✳ Bobbie Takashima

This pattern may be hand-traced or photocopied for personal use only.
Enlarge at 133% to bring it to full size.

Materials

JO SONJA'S ARTIST'S GOUACHE

ANTIQUE GREEN

AQUA

BRILLIANT GREEN

BROWN EARTH

BURGUNDY

CARBON BLACK

DIOXAZINE PURPLE

JAUNE BRILLIANT

MOSS GREEN

NAPTHOL RED
LIGHT

NIMBUS GREY

PACIFIC BLUE

PURPLE MADDER

RAW SIENNA

RAW UMBER

SMOKED PEARL

TITANIUM WHITE

ULTRAMARINE BLUE

YELLOW LIGHT

SURFACE

- ꩜ wooden pie box by
  Country Pleasures

ROYAL & LANGNICKEL AQUALON BRUSHES

- ꩜ no. 8 filbert
- ꩜ no. 10/0 liner
- ꩜ 3-inch (76mm) prep
- ꩜ nos. 2, 6 round
- ꩜ no. 20 short round
- ꩜ ¾-inch (19mm) wash

ADDITIONAL SUPPLIES

- ꩜ American Traditional stencils
  BL-130 snowflakes
  MS-162 snowflakes
- ꩜ gray graphite paper
- ꩜ Jo Sonja's Clear Glazing Medium
- ꩜ Jo Sonja's Kleister Medium
- ꩜ J.W. etc. White Lightning
- ꩜ stylus

RAW SURFACE ▼

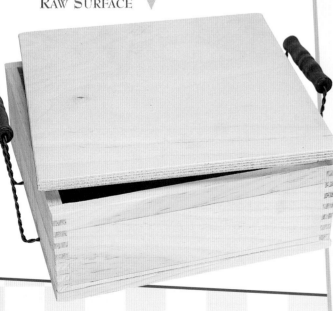

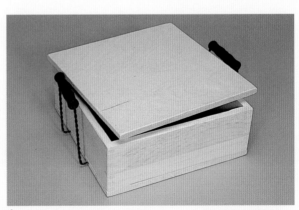

1 Prepare the surface with a coat of White Lightning. Transfer the pattern using gray graphite paper and a stylus. Then, prepare a very loose brush mix of Burgundy + Napthol Red Light + Kleister Medium. Apply a very uneven coat of this mix with a 3-inch (76mm) brush to give depth right away.

Snowflakes

2 Use a no. 20 short round brush to drybrush, swirl and pounce in the snowflakes using the snowflake stencils. Use a mix of Kleister Medium + Nimbus Grey to fill up the edges and corners to give you a circle in the center of the box. Apply the large snowflakes first, then medium and finally, the smallest.

3 With the same dirty brush, repeat the process with a mix of Smoked Pearl + Kleister. Apply this set of snowflakes in a slightly smaller area. You can even overlap the snowflakes to create more depth.

4 Repeat the above process again with Titanium White on the dirty brush. This time apply only the tiniest stars or flakes.

5 Your box should look similar to this. Now you're ready to apply the pattern.

Snowman & Jack Frost

6 Brush sketch the snowman and Jack Frost in the shadow areas with Purple Madder using a no. 6 round. I call this *shadow painting*. Scrub in the color using the side of the brush.

7 Fill in the snowman and Jack Frost using Pacific Blue + Kleister Medium with a no. 20 short round. Scrub with the side of the brush, filling in the space and following the pattern lines. Allow the Purple Madder shading to show through.

8 Paint for a soft-edged effect by adding Pacific Blue + Kleister Medium. Don't fill in as much as you did previously. Add this mix to the outer edges of the trees using a no. 8 filbert brush. Keep it light and soft. Think airflow.

9 Start in the highlight area with Nimbus Grey. You'll need to scrub this color in to keep it light and soft. Add Antique Green to the trees.

10 Apply Smoked Pearl as you did Nimbus Grey but to a smaller area to build the color. Using a dirty brush, base the nose with Burgundy and the twig arms with Brown Earth. With a mix of Kleister Medium + Carbon Black on the dirty brush, pull in from the sides of the hat to the highlighted area. Add a little more Smoked Pearl on Jack Frost.

Snowman & Jack Frost, *continued*

11 Add highlights to the trees with the dirty brush plus Moss Green. Use less mix as you move toward the background. Add Raw Sienna to the snowman's arms and Napthol Red Light to his nose. Mix Aqua + Titanium White, and add it to the snowman's hat. With the same mix, paint the back corner of Jack Frost's eye.

12 With a 10/0 liner, apply a thinned mix of Titanium White + Raw Sienna to the snowman's arms. Mix Yellow Light + Titanium White and highlight the nose. Use Brown Earth for the snowman's buttons, eyes and mouth. Put Brown Earth on the eyes, nose and tree mouths. Paint Jack's pupil with a mix of Raw Umber + Carbon Black, and dab his teeth with Nimbus Grey. With a liner brush, add Antique Green to the hatband.

13 Mix Jaune Brilliant + Yellow Light + Titanium White for Jack Frost's flesh. Start with the nose, cheeks, eyelids, forehead, upper and lower lips, earlobe, right hand, and add just a little on the left hand. Add a little Kleister Medium to this mix, and glaze a little on the snowman's cheeks and chin and put an accent on the middle of his body. Shade the bottom of the snowman's nose and the bottoms and backs of the arms. Highlight the trees with a mix of Yellow Light + Titanium White + Moss Green + Brilliant Green. Apply this mix to the tree's facial features, too.

14 Mix Titanium White with a touch of Yellow Light + water, and add the final highlight to the tips of Jack Frost's nose, teeth, suit and icicles. Add the eye highlight at ten o'clock. Highlight the snowman on the right side, buttons, eyes and teeth with Yellow Light + Titanium White. Mix Pacific Blue + Kleister on the left side of the trees and where the trees meet. Soften the ground with dabs and swirls. Some should go clockwise, and others should go counterclockwise for contrast.

Snowflake Faeries

15 Loosely brush mix Smoked Pearl + Titanium White + a touch of Kleister Medium. Add small snowflakes circling the snowman and Jack Frost. Jack is pulling them out of his sack and letting them go over the snowman. There is a special faerie in the snowman's hand.

16 Use straight Jaune Brilliant to dab on the heads and bodies of the faeries, working them into the snowflake. The legs and arms come from the center of the flake. To create movement, bend the arms and legs.

17 Shade the faerie bodies, legs and arms with Purple Madder using a no. 2 round brush. These are simple strokes along the back and bottom edges, away from the light coming from the center of the design.

18 Highlight the faeries using the no. 2 round brush loaded with a mix of Yellow Light + Titanium White. Put little tornadoes on top of their heads for hairdos.

Final Details

19 Dress the ¾-inch (19mm) wash brush in Kleister Medium. Pick up Nimbus Grey. Make short swirly strokes, barely touching the surface. Think air movement and blowing snow. Break the edge of the snowman. Use Smoked Pearl + a touch of Titanium White to continue the swirls. Add tiny snowflakes in the center.

20 Mix Clear Glazing Medium + Ultramarine Blue Deep. Glaze in from the side with this very thin wash of color. Walk it in from the edges toward the center.

21 Using the same dirty brush, add Dioxazine Purple thinned with Clear Glazing Medium. Add a little on the edges and corners of the surface but less than the blue mix. Don't bring it into the center too much. Apply to your taste.

Completed Lid

The Boo Box

The inspiration for this outrageous design comes naturally as I reminisce about bygone days in my town—pumpkin fields, farms and critters coming out to play on Halloween night. My sisters and I are in the background, trick-or-treating house-to-house in the moonlight.

The techniques used in this design are two of my favorites: drybrushing and glazing. The drybrushing with the broken coverage of paint creates soft edges and texture. The glaze adds exciting color and interest and it's a tool to carry color for balance and harmony.

Enjoy the process of building the design in layers. Feel free to stroke beyond the pattern lines.

Here's to the good ol' days…

Happy haunting!

Pattern

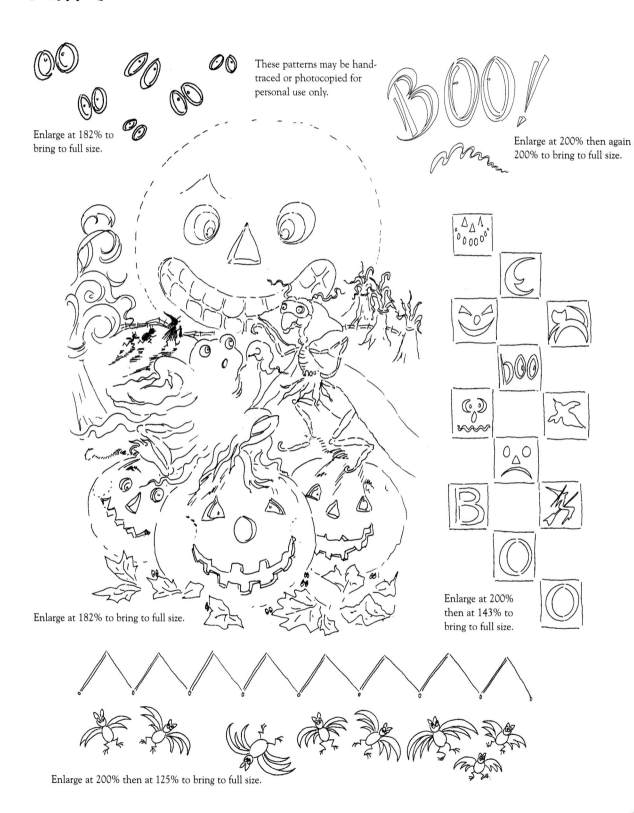

These patterns may be hand-traced or photocopied for personal use only.

Enlarge at 182% to bring to full size.

BOO!

Enlarge at 200% then again 200% to bring to full size.

Enlarge at 182% to bring to full size.

Enlarge at 200% then at 143% to bring to full size.

Enlarge at 200% then at 125% to bring to full size.

Materials

Jo Sonja's Artist's Gouache

 AMETHYST

 AQUA

 BRILLIANT GREEN

 BROWN EARTH

 BURGUNDY

 CARBON BLACK

  CHARCOAL

 COBALT BLUE

DIOXAZINE PURPLE

MOSS GREEN

NAPTHOL RED LIGHT

NIMBUS GREY

PACIFIC BLUE

PALE GOLD METALLIC

SMOKED PEARL

TITANIUM WHITE

   TRANSPARENT MAGENTA

  VERMILION

  YELLOW LIGHT

YELLOW OXIDE

Surface

- wooden makeup box by Country Pleasures

Royal & Langnickel Aqualon Brushes

- nos. 6, 8 filbert
- nos. 2, 10/0 liner
- nos. 2, 4 round
- ¾-inch (19mm) wash

Royal & Langnickel Royal Sable Brushes

- no. 8 or 10 duster
- 1-inch (25mm) flat

Additional Supplies

- chalk pencil
- gray graphite paper
- Jo Sonja's Clear Glazing Medium
- Jo Sonja's Kleister Medium
- stylus

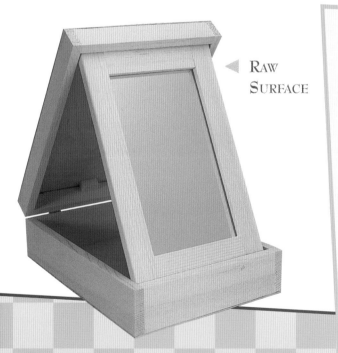

◀ RAW SURFACE

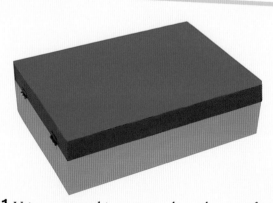

1 Using gray graphite paper and a stylus, transfer the pattern. Using a ¾-inch (19mm) wash brush, basecoat the box with Charcoal on the lid and top sides and Vermilion on the bottom sides. Make sure the paint is thick and applied in a choppy manner.

Bottom & Top Sides of Box

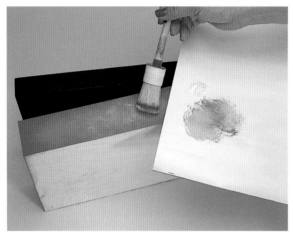

2 Dress the brush in Vermilion. Then pick up Yellow Light + a little Kleister Medium and loosely mix on your palette by stippling. Apply Yellow Light using a duster brush to the center area of each side.

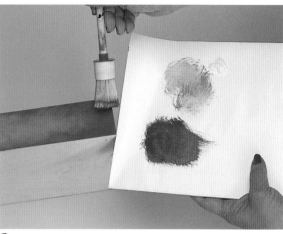

3 Using the dirty brush + Burgundy + a little bit of Kleister Medium, again pounce on your palette and apply to the edges of each side.

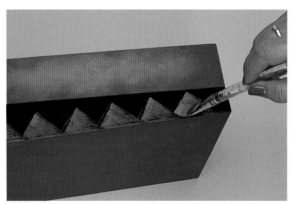

4 Mark off every inch (25mm) on the side of the lid using a chalk pencil. Using a 1-inch (25mm) flat brush loaded with Amethyst + a little Kleister Medium, apply the triangles with the dry-brush technique. The ends will have only half triangles.

5 Drybrush a line of Yellow Light on the right side of the triangles, using a no. 2 or 3 round brush.

Tee-Hee Tip

Wipe the brush if you get too much paint on it. Otherwise, just use the dirty brush for your painting.

Bats

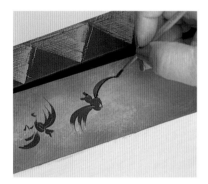

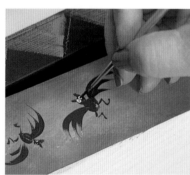

6 With a no. 2 liner brush fully loaded with Carbon Black, begin to paint the bats on the sides of the box.

7 When you apply color, allow the underneath colors to show through. The head of the bat is a circle, the body is egg shaped, the ears are triangles and the wings are sloppy **C**-strokes.

8 Pull the wings out from the side of the body.

9 The feet are little lines underneath the body, and don't forget the little toes.

10 Paint the eyeballs with a mix of Titanium White + a touch of Yellow Light. Make little oval shapes, using very little pressure.

11 Add a tiny dot of Carbon Black to the center of the yellow eyes. Feel free to use a smaller liner brush if you need to.

12 Load the no. 2 liner brush with a mix of Yellow Light + a touch of Brilliant Green + a touch of Titanium White. Add a line over the original Yellow Light line on the left side of the triangles. Add another line with a mix of Vermilion + Yellow Light.

Trick-or-Treaters

13 For the *boo* eyes, basecoat Carbon Black oval shapes with a no. 6 filbert and then stroke them with a no. 2 round loaded with Amethyst. Add Pacific Blue strokes, and then highlight with a mix of Yellow Light + Titanium White (1:1).

Basecoat the word *boo* with Pacific Blue using a no. 8 filbert. Then add Amethyst followed by a mix of Yellow Light + Titanium White (1:1). Finally, highlight the eyes with Titanium White + a touch of Yellow Light.

Paint the hill with Brilliant Green. Go over that with a mix of Brilliant Green + Yellow Light (1:1) and then with that same mix lightened with a touch of Titanium White.

Use a no. 2 round to sketch in the trick-or-treater "stick man" bodies in Carbon Black. Next, paint clothing, hair and other details over the stick bodies. Then use Kleister-thinned black to put in the fence and misshapen shadows under the figures.

Moon Face

14 Basecoat the moon face in Cobalt Blue + a touch of Clear Glazing Medium using a ¾-inch (19mm) wash brush. Use a no. 6 filbert loaded with Nimbus Grey for the eyes and the sides and center of the nose. With a no. 8 filbert, stroke from the outside edge of the teeth toward the lip line, fading out. Load a no. 2 round with a mix of Dioxazine Purple + Pacific Blue for the cornstalk.

Build more color on the face with Pacific Blue. Overstroke the base with Smoked Pearl, using shorter strokes. Add Brown Earth to the pupil area. Paint the nose with Smoked Pearl. Brush Smoked Pearl onto the teeth, using more paint toward the center of the head. With a no. 2 round, stroke Amethyst onto the left sides of the cornstalks.

15 Next, drybrush Aqua onto the face. Glaze Moss Green, Vermilion and Amethyst on the eyes. Add a black pupil to each eye. Glaze Moss Green and Brown Earth on the nose. Glaze Brilliant Green and a touch of Vermilion on the center front area of the teeth and Amethyst and Dioxazine Purple around the lip line edge. Add Yellow Oxide + a touch of Amethyst to the left side of the cornstalk folk.

Apply Moss Green + a touch of Smoked Pearl to the face. Use Amethyst to put accent strokes onto cheeks and eyebrows. With a mix of Titanium White + Yellow Light (1:1), highlight the dot on the pupil of the eye. Stroke Brown Earth + Dioxazine Purple along the lower edge of the eye area. Darken the left corner and inside area of the nose with Brown Earth + Dioxazine Purple mix. Shade the teeth along the lip line with the same mix. Highlight the cornstalk folk on the left side with a touch of Yellow Light + Titanium White.

Jack-o'-Lantern Grouping

16 For the frog, basecoat the eyes in Brilliant Green + a touch of Yellow Light, the mouth and legs in Brilliant Green and the ghost costume in Dioxazine Purple.

Basecoat the ant's eyes in Titanium White + Yellow Light, its body in Burgundy and its cape in Dioxazine Purple.

Use Burgundy to basecoat the pumpkins and Brown Earth for the stems and leaves.

17 Next, put Smoked Pearl on the frog's costume, pulling strokes from right to left. Top that off with an Amethyst glaze. Apply **C**-strokes to the left sides of his pupils with a mix of Titanium White + Yellow Light and put a Carbon Black oval dot on the pupils. Paint the frog's tongue with a mix of Vermilion + Yellow Light + Titanium White (1:2:1). Dot its legs with Yellow Light + Titanium White (1:1), and glaze Amethyst on the bottom of its foot and along the left sides of its legs and feet.

Paint the ant's cape with a mix of Amethyst + Yellow Light + Titanium White (1:1:1). Line Brilliant Green to form a spoke in its eyes, and use Pacific Blue along the edges of the mask and between the eye holes. Use Napthol Red Light + Vermilion (1:2) for the body.

Add Napthol Red Light + Vermilion to the pumpkin faces and a mix of Vermilion + Yellow Light + Titanium White (1:2:1) to the cutout edges. Put a mix of Brown Earth + Titanium White + Yellow Oxide (1:1:2) on the stems.

Finally, put a Burgundy glaze on a few of the leaves.

18 (Left) Paint the frog's costume Nimbus Grey and the irises of its eyes Brown Earth. Dab Burgundy on the upper right area of its mouth. Dot its legs with a mix of Brilliant Green + Yellow Light (1:1).

Paint the ant's cape with Dioxazine Purple + Amethyst (1:1). Stroke Amethyst on the right side of the eyes. Add Napthol Red Light to the body.

Paint the pumpkin faces with Napthol Red Light, the cutout features with Vermilion and the stems with Brown Earth + Smoked Pearl (1:1).

Put a Brown Earth + Yellow Oxide mix (1:1) on the leaves.

19 (Right) Working wet-on-dry, put a Vermilion glaze and a touch of Burgundy over the left side of the frog's eyes. Dot the pupil with Titanium White + Yellow Light (1:1). Use a Carbon Black liner around the eye and the rim of the mouth. Use a touch of Yellow Light + Titanium White on the tip of the tongue. Glaze the costume with Yellow Light, a touch of Napthol Red Light, Pacific Blue, then Dioxazine Purple. Put tiny brush dots of Yellow Light + Titanium White (1:2) on the frog's legs.

Glaze the ant's cape with Pacific Blue, and line with Yellow Light + Titanium White. Highlight the mask with Aqua + Titanium White. Highlight and line the body with a mix of + Yellow Light + White (1:2:1).

Line the pumpkin faces and cutouts with a mix of Yellow Light + Titanium White. Put a glaze of Translucent Magenta on the nose and mouth holes and along the edges of the teeth. Accent the lower teeth with Amethyst + Dioxazine Purple (1:1). Stroke the eyes and dot the pupils with a mix of Yellow Light + Titanium White.

Put a few strokes of Yellow Oxide + Smoked Pearl along the leaf edges and apply Yellow Oxide + Titanium White ovals to the *boo* eyes and dot the pupils with Carbon Black.

Final Touches

20 Loosely mix and thin Kleister Medium + Pacific Blue + Dioxazine Purple. Apply this mix to the box on the edges in a swirling motion, pulling toward you. Apply one coat of Clear Glazing Medium.

21 Add a gold dot at the peak of the triangle using Pale Gold Metallic thinned with water.

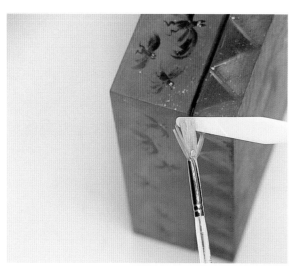

22 Spatter thinned Pale Gold Metallic by tapping off the excess and pulling up on the brush with a palette knife. Spatter out and forward.

Tee-Hee Tip

A short pull will give you smaller spatters and a heavy long stroke will give you larger spatters.

Completed Box

▲ LID

INSIDE ▲

▲ SIDE

7

The Pumpkin Carver

For this piece, I decided to try a different approach to the Halloween color scheme. Rather than a dark background, I've chosen to work on a light-value background, adding just enough dark values for contrast and to make the details interesting.

I'm using a very old "rub out" technique, popular with many artists. Today, with the addition of retarder to the surface and paint, the drying process slows and the extended open time makes it easier for us to create our designs—especially spooky ones!

Pattern

This pattern may be hand-traced or photocopied for personal use only. Enlarge at 147% to bring it to full size.

Materials

Jo Sonja's Artist's Gouache

AQUA

BRILLIANT GREEN

BURGUNDY

CARBON BLACK

NAPTHOL RED LIGHT

NORWEGIAN ORANGE

PACIFIC BLUE

PURPLE MADDER

RAW SIENNA

RAW UMBER

SMOKED PEARL

TITANIUM WHITE

VERMILION

YELLOW LIGHT

Surface

- wooden cabinet by Country Pleasures

Royal & Langnickel Aqualon Brushes

- no. 4 filbert
- nos. 2, 4 round
- ¾-inch (19mm) round
- ½-inch (12mm) wash

Royal & Langnickel Royal Fusion Brushes

- no. 8 filbert
- no. 2 round

Royal & Langnickel Royal Sable Brushes

- no. 8 duster
- 1-inch (25mm) flat

Additional Supplies

- gray graphite paper
- Jo Sonja's Clear Glazing Medium
- Jo Sonja's Kleister Medium
- Jo Sonja's Retarder Medium
- medium-grit sandpaper
- paper towel
- stylus

◀ RAW SURFACE

Brush Sketching

1 Moisten the door with retarder. You can use your hand to spread it over the surface. Don't apply too much retarder; it should look like matte varnish. Give it a minute to soak in. If you have too much, your paint will bleed over the surface. We want the paint to glide over the surface and maintain an edge.

Transfer the pattern. Use gray graphite paper and a stylus.

Brush sketch the entire design with a no. 2 round with a brush mix of Kleister Medium + Raw Sienna. Erase the graphite lines if needed.

2 Prepare the rest of the surface with a "veil" of retarder. No puddles, please. The porosity of the wood will dictate the need for another coat or not.

3 Start with a little retarder in a ¾-inch (19mm) brush. Side-load with Yellow Light and slip-slap in the center of interest.

4 Change to a ½-inch (12mm) oval wash brush. Dress it in retarder and side-load in Norwegian Orange. Add choppy strokes to the orange areas for the flicker of light and luminosity.

5 Pause. Evaluate the light-to-dark contrast at this point. This technique of layering translucent pigments is the backbone of your design. You will get the most information about the design at this stage.

6 Using a no. 4 round brush loaded with Purple Madder, shade the pumpkin and faerie by brush sketching to create form.

7 Add more contrast by mixing Purple Madder + Carbon Black. Using the no. 2 round brush, add to the shaded areas. Concentrate on the value gradation. Let this dry.

9 Using retarder + Norwegian Orange, start at the edges of the cabinet and pull into the center using the dry-brush technique.

8 Apply Clear Glazing Medium + Norwegian Orange for a warm color around the door frame. Use the dry-brush technique. (See page 6.)

Tee-Hee Tip

If your brush gets dry, add a touch of retarder.

Faeries

10 Base the face, hands and fingers with Titanium White + a touch of Norwegian Orange. This should not be very detailed. The color should be three values darker than the background. Shade the back of the head, chin, turned-up nose, bottom side of the hand and fingers with a mix of Norwegian Orange + Purple Madder. The mouth is in an oval for a surprised look.

11 Apply Carbon Black on damp retarder to the edges of the wings, the hair, the mask, where the wings meet the body, the pants, the dress, the inside of the pumpkin, the candle sconce, the left side of the candle and the lower right side of the pumpkin. Walk in the black for a gradation of color. Clean your brush.

12 While the retarder is wet, use thinned Pacific Blue and work it into the background with a large flat brush especially on the shadow side. Work it in and out of the wings for color.

Spooky Witch

13 Over the retarder, slip-slap Raw Umber + a touch of Carbon Black in the upper half of the door. You will lose your pattern, but a witch can't be too ugly, so don't worry about the pattern. Of course, if you don't like it, wipe it off and start over. Don't make the witch any darker than this; she isn't your focal point.

14 While the surface is still wet, slip-slap in a little Carbon Black where the witch's face will be.

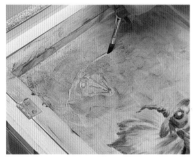

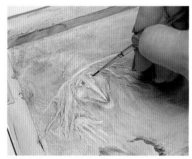

15 Dampen a no. 4 filbert with water. Blot it dry and begin to wipe out the witch's face. Have the pattern handy so you can refer to it. The nose is a long string bean and the nostrils are like peas. Make a letter **T** to form the forehead and eyeballs. Lift off more in the highpoint areas of the face. Connect the highpoints with fuzzy edges. Press, pull and wiggle to create the fingers. Wipe out the hat so it fades away. Refine the witch's face with a small water-dampened round brush as the retarder begins to feel tacky. I like this stage the best. They don't call me *"Tacky-shima"* for nothing!

16 Before applying *fresh* retarder over *tacky* retarder, be sure to dry the surface completely with a hair dryer. Reapply retarder to the surface, but make sure it's not too wet. Blot it with a paper towel. Using a no. 4 filbert brush fully loaded with Smoked Pearl, touch the highpoints of the witch's face (forehead, eyes, chin and nose) and hat. If the paint begins to dry, touch the brush in retarder. Use a no. 2 round brush loaded with a mix of Smoked Pearl + Titanium White to highlight further.

17 Add the pupil with a mix of retarder + Raw Umber. Add a little detail to the lost edges—but not too much.

Spooky Witch, *continued*

18 Wipe out the smoke coming out of the pumpkin using a no. 8 filbert brush.

19 Add a little bit of the Smoked Pearl to the witch's hands using the no. 2 round brush.

20 Highlight the smoke with Smoked Pearl, using a no. 8 filbert brush.

Pumpkin Faerie

21 Basecoat the hat with glaze-thinned Vermilion. Fill in the edges of the pumpkin's features with Vermilion. Brush a glaze of Yellow Light over the pumpkin. Stroke Vermilion + a touch of glaze from the edges to the center of the pumpkin. Next, use Napthol Red Light, making sure to overlap the Vermilion in the shaded areas.

Stroke glaze-thinned Raw Sienna on the shoes, knife handle and pumpkin stem.

Base the wings with a thin layer of Yellow Light + a touch of Clear Glazing Medium. The cat's nose is a triangle shape of Norwegian Orange + Titanium White (1:1). Basecoat the cat and faerie eyes with a mix of Titanium White + Yellow Light (1:1). Use a mix of Vermilion + Yellow Light (1:1) for the candle flame.

Darken the pumpkin's eyes, nose and mouth with glaze-thinned Raw Umber applied with a no. 2 round. Strengthen the thin black areas with Raw Umber + a touch of Clear Glazing Medium.

22 Add a few streaks of Pacific Blue on the faerie's hair, mask, clothing, candle, sconce and on the right side of the pumpkin. Add Napthol Red Light + Clear Glazing Medium over the shaded areas (left side) of the hat, and apply a touch to the corners of the pumpkin's eyes, nose and mouth.

Next, add Brilliant Green to the faerie's and cat's eyes, and the stripes on the legs. Add a touch to accent the shoes, candle and the left side of the pumpkin. Stroke Norwegian Orange onto the wings in an oval shape. Dab a highlight on the candle flame with Yellow Light + Titanium White (1:1). Line the wick with Raw Umber.

Pumpkin Faerie, *continued*

23 Apply Burgundy over the shaded areas of the hat and pumpkin to darken the red-orange hue. Dab the pupils with a no. 2 round loaded with Carbon Black. Put Aqua + Titanium White (1:1) highlights on the wings, hair, mask, clothing, candle, sconce and knife blade.

Touch the center of the candle flame with Napthol Red Light. Highlight the candle wax with a mix of Yellow Light + Titanium White (1:1). Base the pumpkins on the faerie's clothing with Norwegian Orange.

24 Apply highlights of Yellow Light + Titanium White (1:1) on the faerie's face, hair and clothing, and on the pumpkin, candle sconce, candle, knife and the glow around the candle flame.

Highlight the pumpkins of the dress with a touch of Vermilion + Yellow Light (1:1). Dot the facial features with a liner brush loaded with Raw Umber.

Paint the pumpkin shavings covering the ground very casually with slip-slap strokes using a no. 8 filbert loaded with Purple Madder.

Sides

25 Apply retarder to the sides of the cabinet. Work on one side at a time since this is a wipe-out technique that is a bit easier to wipe out while tacky.

26 Using a 1-inch (25mm) flat brush loaded with Norwegian Orange, apply the checks. Apply to only about one-third of the surface. The checks can be any color on your palette. I've chosen orange as the dominant color.

27 Oops! If the paint begins to bleed, wipe it up with a dry brush, paper towel or your finger. Let the retarder set a little longer to avoid this problem.

28 Using a water-dampened brush, wipe out child-like shapes and words. Wipe on a towel. If you don't like what you've done, wipe it off the surface and start over. Any Halloween symbol is fine. Let it dry flat. Apply a coat or two of Clear Glazing Medium before varnishing. This glaze is used as a barrier coat for the Kleister Medium + retarder mix so that it won't lift during the varnishing step.

Final Touches

29 You may drybrush a final "spooky" antiquing to the edges of the cabinet in Purple Madder. A touch of Raw Umber may by drybrushed onto the design with a ¾-inch (19mm) glaze brush or the no. 3 duster brush. Happy hauntings!

CLOSE-UP OF THE SPOOKY WITCH

COMPLETED CABINET ▲

Creepy Garden People

Once a year, without fear,
The veggie people gather here.
Laughing, dancing, from dusk to dawn
On this day...October thirty-one!
                    Tee-hee!

This project's painting technique is a personal favorite: drybrushing. The effect is casual, soft, textured...interesting! I also like the idea of the dark background peeking through the painting and strengthening the darkest values of the painting. This dark from the background actually saves us a painting step.

A gradual building of values, hues (especially the hue's temperature) and chroma (intensity) is slow at times but very relaxing—no rush to the finish. Enjoy the process.

Pattern

This pattern may be hand-traced or photocopied for personal use only. Join the pattern below at the dashed lines. Enlarge all patterns at 200% and then at 125% to bring them to full size.

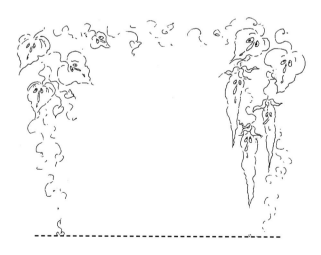

Materials

Jo Sonja's Artist's Gouache

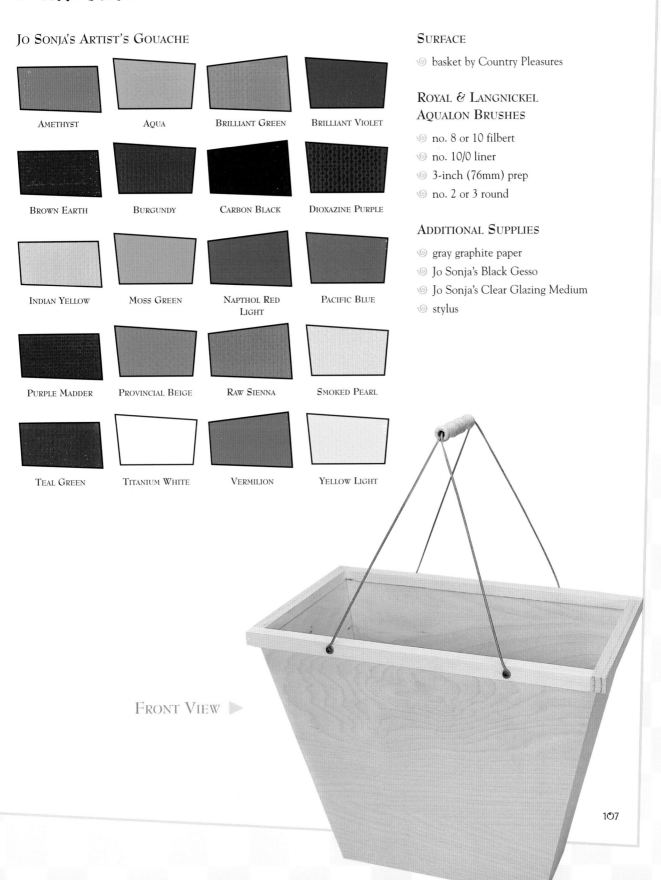

AMETHYST	AQUA	BRILLIANT GREEN	BRILLIANT VIOLET
BROWN EARTH	BURGUNDY	CARBON BLACK	DIOXAZINE PURPLE
INDIAN YELLOW	MOSS GREEN	NAPTHOL RED LIGHT	PACIFIC BLUE
PURPLE MADDER	PROVINCIAL BEIGE	RAW SIENNA	SMOKED PEARL
TEAL GREEN	TITANIUM WHITE	VERMILION	YELLOW LIGHT

Surface

◉ basket by Country Pleasures

Royal & Langnickel Aqualon Brushes

◉ no. 8 or 10 filbert
◉ no. 10/0 liner
◉ 3-inch (76mm) prep
◉ no. 2 or 3 round

Additional Supplies

◉ gray graphite paper
◉ Jo Sonja's Black Gesso
◉ Jo Sonja's Clear Glazing Medium
◉ stylus

FRONT VIEW ▷

Preparing the Surface & Basecoating

1 Apply a coat of Jo Sonja's Black Gesso with a 3-inch (76mm) prep brush. Basecoat the background in Black Gesso. Before the gesso dries, casually streak in some Teal Green. Dry. Transfer the pattern.

Tee-Hee Tip

For this project, I did not add any mediums to the pigment. I used a 10/0 liner for the linework, a no. 2 round for the small areas and a no. 10 filbert brush for the large areas.

La Raw Onion

2 For La Raw Onion, use a no. 10 filbert for the large spaces, a no. 2 round for small ones and a 10/0 liner for final dots and details.

Basecoat the head and hair with a mix of Pacific Blue + Brown Earth + a touch of Smoked Pearl. Make a U-shape for the eyes in Smoked Pearl, and use a Burgundy liner for the mouth. Paint the collar and body with Brilliant Green + Teal Green (1:1), and use Brown Earth for the arms and legs.

Then apply Smoked Pearl to the head and hair and Yellow Light + Titanium White to the eyes. Paint the mouth Napthol Red Light and the collar and body Brilliant Green. Use Raw Sienna for the arms and legs.

Follow that with Smoked Pearl + a touch of Titanium White for the head and hair and Vermilion + Yellow Light for the lips. Paint the collar and body Brilliant Green + Moss Green. Apply strokes of Moss Green + Yellow Light (1:1) to the arms and legs and a touch of Vermilion to the left sides of the black pupils.

Use a Carbon Black liner for the eyebrows, eyelash line, top of the lip line and left side of the fangs.

Then add color to the white underpainting, starting with Yellow Light on the right side of the cheeks, nose and chin. Add a touch of Burgundy to the lower side of the cheeks, nose and chin. Softly brush Pacific Blue onto the left side of the head and facial features. Then put on a bit of Amethyst. Add a few Burgundy "spikes" to the eyes to make them look bloodshot and put in a highlight dot with Yellow Light + Titanium White (1:1). Use a Titanium White liner on the fangs and the top of the head, eyebrows, eyelids and eyelashes. Add Pacific Blue and Amethyst accents to the left sides of the leaves and body shapes and drybrush Yellow Light + Titanium White (1:1) highlights to the right front and on the collar, arms and legs.

Finally, dot the body with Brown Earth, then Yellow Light + Titanium White.

Spud Sister & Stalkers

3 The Spud Sister has a basecoat of Brown Earth on his body and oval rings of Provincial Beige for the eyes. Be careful to leave the black background in the pupils exposed. The mouth and carrot legs are Burgundy.

Then put Provincial Beige on the body. Lighten the eyes with Yellow Light + a touch of Titanium White. Lighten the mouth and legs with Napthol Red Light.

Paint the body with a mix of Indian Yellow + Smoked Pearl (1:1), and add a highlight dot of Titanium White + Yellow Light (1:1) to the eyes. Add Vermilion to the mouth and legs, and dab the teeth with Smoked Pearl.

Finally, add linework highlights with Titanium White + a touch of Yellow Light. Brush the body with Vermilion and then a touch of Burgundy. Add Pacific Blue accents on the shadow side of the body parts.

4 Basecoat the Stalkers with Raw Sienna for the bodies and oval rings of Titanium White for the eyes. Use a mix of Teal Green + Moss Green (1:1) for the husks and Burgundy for the mouth openings.

Add Indian Yellow + a touch of Titanium White to the bodies and Amethyst to the eyes. Apply Moss Green + Brilliant Green to the husks, and dab a touch of Napthol Red Light + Vermilion to the mouths.

Then put Yellow Light + Titanium White (1:1) on the bodies, and brush dot the pupils with Carbon Black. Add Yellow Light + Titanium White to the husks and Vermilion + Yellow Light + a touch of Titanium White to the mouths. Underscore the linework on the eyebrows, eyes, noses and mouths in Carbon Black.

Finally, highlight with Yellow Light + Titanium White. Build with several layers, if necessary, in order to add "punch." Add a blush of Napthol Red Light to the corn kernels.

Pepper Pot & Devil-Shrooms

5 Basecoat the green areas of the Pepper Pot with Teal Green + Brilliant Green (1:1). Use Indian Yellow for the eyes. Paint the mouth with Burgundy and the teeth with Smoked Pearl.

Then apply a mix of Brilliant Green + Moss Green on the green areas and Yellow Light + a touch of Titanium White on the eyes. Apply Napthol Red Light on the mouth.

Next, apply Moss Green + Yellow Light + a touch of Titanium White on the green areas. Stroke Burgundy on the right side of the eyes and a dab on the nose. Casually dab Carbon Black to form a roundish shape on the pupils, and stroke a spiral line from the inside to the outside edge of the eye. Add Vermilion + a touch of Yellow Light to the mouth.

Finally, stroke highlights on the green areas, eyes, mouth and teeth with Yellow Light + Titanium White. Put a touch of Vermilion then Burgundy on the leaves, cheeks, and chin. Add accents of Pacific Blue on the left side of the pot and Aqua on the right side.

6 For the Devil-Shrooms, basecoat the heads with Burgundy + Amethyst (1:1) and the stems with Amethyst. Use Raw Sienna to base the arms, legs and tails.

Next, add Napthol Red Light to the faces and horns and highlight the stems, arms and legs with Yellow Light + Titanium White (1:1).

Add Napthol Red Light + a touch of Titanium White to the heads, and shade in the stem backs with Dioxazine Purple. Paint the arms, legs, eyes, noses and mouths with

dabby linework in Purple Madder.

Finally, highlight the heads with Yellow Light + a touch of Titanium White. Add the final accents to the shadow sides of the heads and stems with a few strokes of Pacific Blue. Highlight the arms, legs, eyes, noses, and mouths with Yellow Light + Titanium White using short, choppy lines.

Bean Folks & Blonde Thing

7 Basecoat the Bean Folks in Teal Green + a touch of Brilliant Green. Next, use a brush mix of the base mix and Moss Green applied on a dirty brush. Then, still using a dirty brush, add Yellow Light + Titanium White (1:1).

Next, stroke on a bit of Pacific Blue on the shaded side of the bean bodies. The eyes are large brush dots of Yellow Light + Titanium White. Stroke the noses and mouths with the same mix. Use Carbon Black for the dots and facial feature details. Mix Moss Green + touch of Titanium White for the linework detail around the leaves and bodies.

8 Paint the body of the Blonde Thing with Raw Sienna and the eyes with a mix of Brilliant Green + Teal Green (1:1). Use Burgundy for the mouth opening.

Next, paint the body in Indian Yellow and the eyes with a mix of Yellow Light + a touch of Titanium White. Apply Napthol Red Light to the center area of the mouth and a mix of Brilliant Green + Moss Green (1:1) to the eyelids, arms and legs.

Paint the body with Yellow Light + a touch of Titanium White and the green area of the eyes with a touch of Brown Earth. Lighten and brighten the center of the mouth with Vermilion + Yellow Light (1:1). Apply Smoked Pearl for teeth. Lighten the arms and legs with Yellow Light + a touch of Titanium White.

Paint the pupils Carbon Black, then highlight with Yellow Light + a dot of Titanium White. Go over

the edges of the teeth with Titanium White + a touch of Yellow Light.

Finally, use a glaze of Vermilion to add blush to the cheeks, nose and chin. Then add a touch of Burgundy to the bottoms of these areas. Brush a bit of Brilliant Violet on the shaded side of the body parts. Use very fine lines of Yellow Light + Titanium White for the final hairy linework.

Pumpkin Gardener & Cally-Flower

9 Start the Pumpkin Gardener by painting the face with a basecoat of Burgundy, and then fill in the eyes and mouth with Purple Madder. Use a mix of Burgundy + Vermilion (1:1) for the carrot nose and a mix of Pacific Blue + Brown Earth (1:1) + a touch of Smoked Pearl for the hat. Paint the leaves and collar of the hat with Teal Green. Dab Smoked Pearl onto the Cally-Flower head, and paint the leaves with a few S- and C-strokes in Teal Green + a touch of Titanium White in a very casual manner.

Next, build stronger light values to the right side of the face, tops of cheeks, jowls, chin, forehead and eyelids with a mix of Burgundy + Vermilion (1:1). Inside the eyes and mouth, use a mix of Vermilion + Napthol Red Light (1:1). Stroke a mix of Pacific Blue + Brown Earth (1:1) to form corn kernel teeth. Stroke Vermilion across the top edge of the carrot nose. Put streaks of Teal Green + Dioxazine Purple (1:1) on the green onion hair. Apply a mix of Pacific Blue + a touch of Titanium White to the hat in streaky strokes. Dab Smoked Pearl + Titanium White on the Cally-Flower face, working from the center out to the edges. Lighten the edges of the leaves closest to her face with a mix of Teal Green+ Moss Green (1:1). Accent the collar and hat leaves with a mix of Brilliant Green + Moss Green (1:1).

Overlap the first level of color on the face with a mix of Vermilion + Indian Yellow (2:1). Apply a C-stroke with a mix of Vermilion + Yellow Light (1:1) to the left side of the eyes and mouth. Add a dabby Carbon Black dot to the pupils and C-strokes of Vermilion + Yellow Light (1:2) at the top of the carrot nose and then Burgundy strokes to the bottom half of the nose. Drybrush Aqua + a touch of Titanium White to the front edge of the hat. Put Moss Green + a touch of Yellow Light on the pumpkin leaves and Moss Green + Brilliant Green (1:1) on the outside edges of the onion hair. Dab in facial features of the Cally-Flower face using Purple Madder with accents of Dioxazine Purple in the shadow areas. Lighten the edges of the Cally leaves with Moss Green + Yellow Light (1:1).

Next, stroke and dab a mix of Vermilion + Yellow Light + Titanium White (1:1:1) onto cheeks, forehead, chin line, eye and mouth.

Add a dot to the pupil. Drybrush Smoked Pearl on the edges of the teeth, and use Yellow Light + Titanium White to highlight the carrot nose. Stroke a squiggly line of Smoked Pearl from the nose to simulate hair. Edge the pumpkin leaves in Smoked Pearl. Streak Moss Green + Yellow Light + Titanium White (1:1:1) on the onion hair. Dab Yellow Light + Titanium White onto the forehead, cheeks, nose and chin. Add Napthol Red Light for blush. Edge the Cally leaves very loosely in Yellow Light + Titanium White. Add lots of squiggly lines of Smoked Pearl + a touch of water to the pumpkin's rooty hair.

Finally, you may want to add glazes of any of the palette colors onto what you've already done for added interest.

Finished Basket

SIDE VIEW ▶

FRONT VIEW ▲

9

Frog Prince & Princess Clock

Long ago and far, far away, there lived a frog in a pond and a princess in her castle…

Well, you've heard the old folk tale of the Frog Prince. It has always been my favorite and it inspired me to design this Frog Prince & Princess Clock. There is, however, a twist to the tale! After the kiss, the princess turned into a frog and they lived happily ever after on the castle pond. I just love hoppy endings. Hope you'll like this one! Toadally!

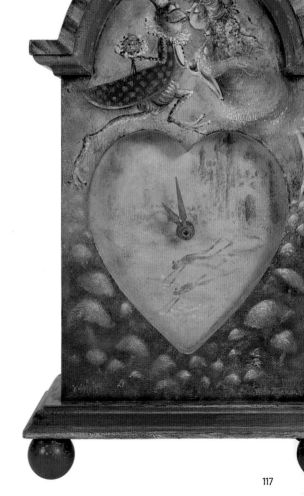

Pattern

These patterns may be hand-traced or photocopied for personal use only. Enlarge at 200% to bring them to full size.

These patterns may be hand-traced or photocopied for personal use only. Enlarge at 153% to bring them to full size.

Materials

Jo Sonja's Artist's Gouache

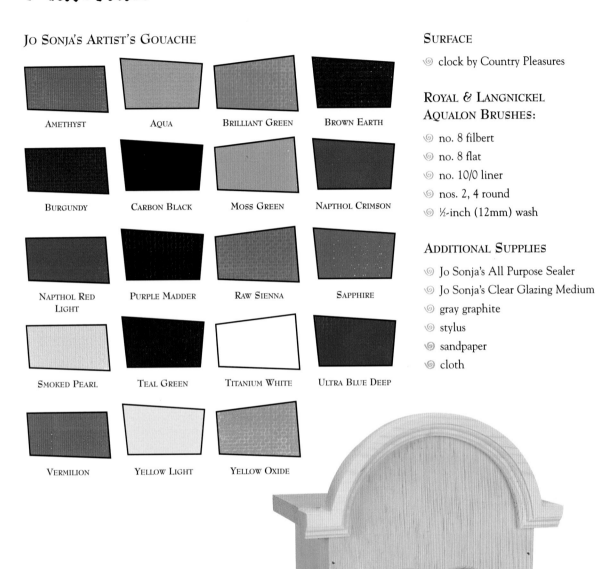

AMETHYST	AQUA	BRILLIANT GREEN	BROWN EARTH
BURGUNDY	CARBON BLACK	MOSS GREEN	NAPTHOL CRIMSON
NAPTHOL RED LIGHT	PURPLE MADDER	RAW SIENNA	SAPPHIRE
SMOKED PEARL	TEAL GREEN	TITANIUM WHITE	ULTRA BLUE DEEP
VERMILION	YELLOW LIGHT	YELLOW OXIDE	

SURFACE

- clock by Country Pleasures

ROYAL & LANGNICKEL AQUALON BRUSHES:

- no. 8 filbert
- no. 8 flat
- no. 10/0 liner
- nos. 2, 4 round
- ½-inch (12mm) wash

ADDITIONAL SUPPLIES

- Jo Sonja's All Purpose Sealer
- Jo Sonja's Clear Glazing Medium
- gray graphite
- stylus
- sandpaper
- cloth

RAW SURFACE ▶

Preparing the Surface

1 Use a ½-inch (12mm) wash brush and base the clock with Teal Green + a touch of all-purpose sealer. Dry. Sand. Wipe with dry cloth. Transfer the pattern using gray graphite and a stylus.

2 Slip-slap Teal Green + Moss Green + Clear Glazing Medium above the clock opening to introduce a warmer color. Let this fade on the edges for a value and intensity gradation.

3 Base the top and bottom trim areas in Burgundy + a touch of Brown Earth. Decorate the front edge of the trim with dark and light stripes. Use a no. 2 round brush and, casually overlapping strokes, drybrush Raw Sienna into Yellow Oxide and then Purple Madder. Again overlap the light stripes and drybrush in Moss Green, then Smoked Pearl and Amethyst. Drybrush the bottom trim with a bit of Napthol Crimson into the Yellow Oxide.

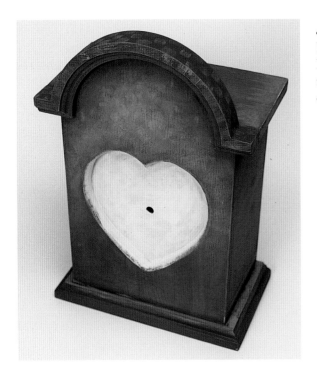

4 Stroke in a casual checked pattern using a no. 8 flat loaded with Napthol Crimson + a touch of Vermilion. Drybrush the blue trim on the ball feet with Ultramarine Blue Deep and then Sapphire. Then put a touch of Amethyst in the center arch.

5 With a no. 8 filbert, casually pit-pat Moss Green + a touch of Smoked Pearl and then add Yellow Oxide and Vermilion.

Frog Prince and Princess

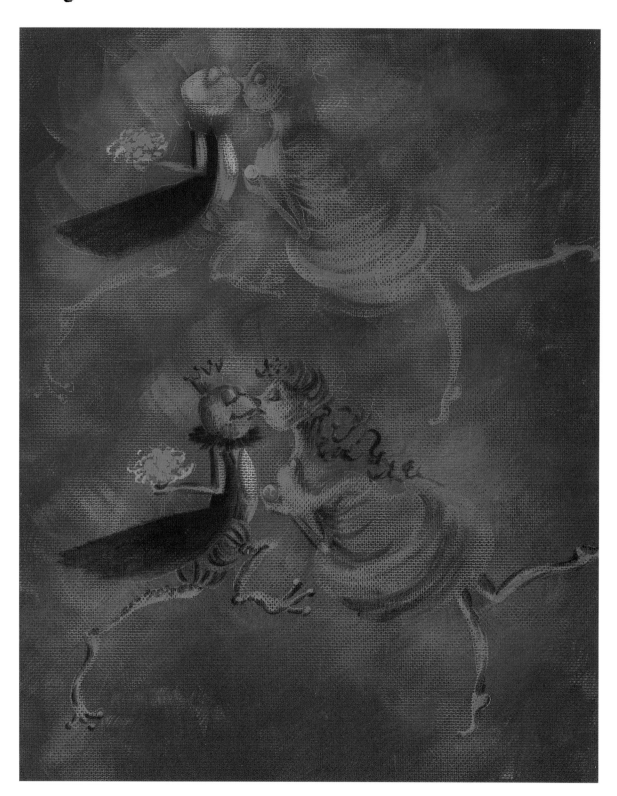

6 Paint the frog flesh a mix of Vermilion + a touch of Titanium White (5:1). Base the crown in Raw Sienna and the coat in Napthol Crimson. His vest is a mix of Sapphire + Napthol Crimson + Titanium White (4:1:1) (hereafter referred to as the blue mix). Paint the shirt and the doily with Smoked Pearl and the pants with Raw Sienna. Dab the nosegay with the blue mix.

Paint the princess's flesh as you did the frog's. Use **C**-strokes in Raw Sienna for her hair. Paint sweeping, casual **C**-strokes with the blue mix for her dress, and base the ball in Yellow Oxide.

7 Load a no. 2 or 4 round with Purple Madder, and apply to the back of shapes and to separate areas that overlap. Dab dots of Amethyst in the center area of the nosegay.

Tee-Hee Tip

Don't worry if your paint mixes aren't in the exact same proportions as mine. These are only a suggestion. Feel free to do your own thing!

Frog Prince & Princess, *continued*

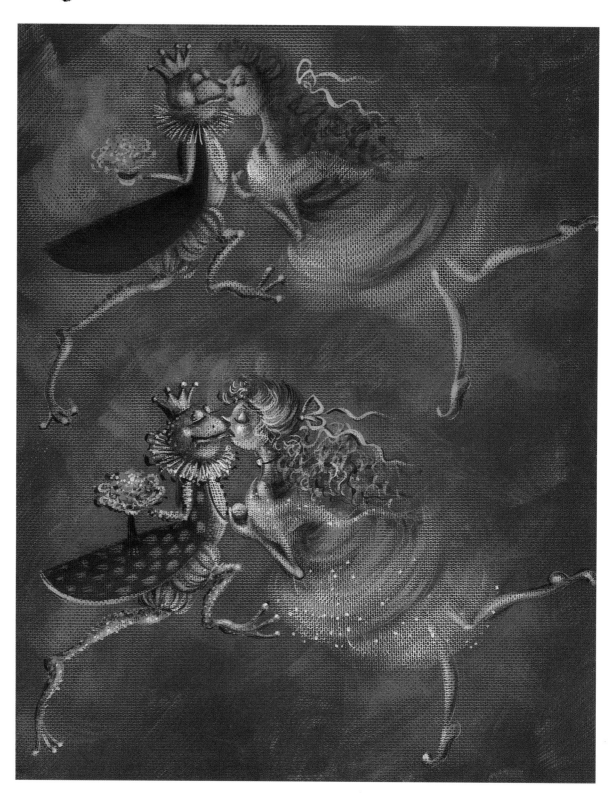

8 Next, build highlights on the front of the flesh areas with a mix of Vermilion + Yellow Light + Titanium White. Apply Yellow Oxide to the crown and Smoked Pearl to the collar with lines simulating the spokes of a wheel. Stroke Napthol Red Light + a touch of Napthol Crimson along the lower edge of the jacket. Use Aqua + a touch of Titanium White for the vest. Stroke the left side of the pants with the blue mix and the right side with Smoked Pearl. Dab dots of Amethyst + Yellow Oxide on the center area of the nosegay.

Highlight the princess's flesh as you did that of the frog and stroke a mix of Burgundy + a touch of Raw Sienna on her hair. Apply Aqua + a touch of Titanium White to her hairbow and Smoked Pearl in sweeping front-to-back strokes for her dress. Dab a touch of Vermilion + Burgundy to the lower half of the ball.

9 Lighten flesh areas of the frog again with Yellow Light + a touch of Titanium White. Dab no. 2 round brush dots of Brilliant Green on the shaded and mid-value areas. Top this off with dots of Aqua + a touch of Titanium White. Softly brush Napthol Red Light onto the cheeks and lower lip, and highlight the crown with Yellow Light + Titanium White. Apply Amethyst + Clear Glazing Medium in a checkered fashion onto the jacket, and then add a few accent touches of Aqua + a touch of Titanium White to the front edges. Apply lines of Titanium White to the shirt, and use Purple Madder for the buttons and liner. Highlight the vest in Aqua + a touch of Titanium White. Use Yellow Light + Titanium White on the front and top areas of the pants and then a few strokes of Aqua + a touch of Titanium White overlapping the blue mix area. Paint Yellow Light + Titanium White dots in the center area of the nosegay and a few squiggly lines and dots around the flowers with a liner loaded with Smoked Pearl + Titanium White (1:1).

The flesh highlights for the princess are as for the frog. Put Napthol Crimson on the lips and cheeks and use a liner loaded with Yellow Light + a touch of Titanium White to add detail to the hair. Highlight the edges of the bow with Aqua + Titanium White (1:1) and use a Carbon Black liner for the choker. Paint the dot with Smoked Pearl topped with a black dot. Using Smoked Pearl + Titanium White (1:1), use sweeping dry brushed strokes for her dress, and sprinkle in a few dots and then more dots in Yellow Light + Titanium White. Put in accent strokes of Aqua + Titanium White (2:1). Dab dots of Yellow Light + Titanium White on top of ball.

Mushrooms

10 The front of the clock has a green background, and the side of the clock has a red and green background. Paint all the mushrooms on the clock with the same hues. The effects change depending on the background.

Basecoat all the mushrooms in Moss Green except for one, which is basecoated in Burgundy. Then shade with a mix of Moss Green and the blue mix. Highlight with Smoked Pearl + a touch of Moss Green and then accent the shaded side with more blue mix. Next, use Burgundy to accent near the highlight and then dance a little Amethyst in the shaded area and midvalues. You may stroke a bit of linework around a few mushrooms, if desired, using a mix of Yellow Light + Titanium White.

Heart Inset

11 Basecoat the heart inset with Smoked Pearl. The design merely suggests shapes in Teal Green + Glazing Medium. Use a small round brush to sketch the scene.

12 Highlight the water and sky area in Smoked Pearl + Titanium White, and then add tints of Aqua + Titanium White over these areas. Dapple the thick edges of the heart cutout in Amethyst and blue mix + water or Clear Glazing Medium. Drybrush the metal clock hands with the blue mix, then Aqua, then Amethyst.

Final Touches

13 A drybrushed antiquing helps to age and soften the corners and edges of the clock. Use a layering of colors. First, apply Purple Madder and then the blue mix to add a soft haze to the edges and sides of the mushrooms.

▲ Finished Front of Clock

10

Santa & the Woodland Elves

A combination of painting techniques to create various effects in this painting made it fun.

I began with a wet-on-wet technique for the background, controlling the texture and intensity of hues by thinning paint with retarder and applying it in soft pit-pat strokes of the brush. The warm faces play off the cool background hues and seem to be washed in moonlight.

The background plays an important part in this moonlight setting, as it comes up through the painting, especially in the shaded areas, to create soft, disappearing edges.

Enjoy the coming of winter!

Pattern

These patterns may be hand-traced or
photocopied for personal use only.
Enlarge at 167% to bring it to full size.

Materials

Jo Sonja's Artist's Gouache

BRILLIANT VIOLET

BROWN EARTH

BURGUNDY

CARBON BLACK

CELADON

DEEP PLUM

DOLPHIN BLUE

GALAXY BLUE

NIMBUS GREY

PACIFIC BLUE

PALE GOLD METALLIC

PROVINCIAL BEIGE

PURPLE MADDER

RAW SIENNA

SMOKED PEARL

TITANIUM WHITE

VERMILION

YELLOW LIGHT

SURFACE

- box by Country Pleasures

ROYAL & LANGNICKEL AQUALON BRUSHES

- no. 8 filbert
- no. 10/0 liner
- no. 2 round
- ¾-inch (19mm) wash

ADDITIONAL SUPPLIES

- gray graphite paper
- Jo Sonja's Clear Glazing Medium
- Jo Sonja's Retarder Medium
- stylus

RAW SURFACE ▶

Preparing the Surface

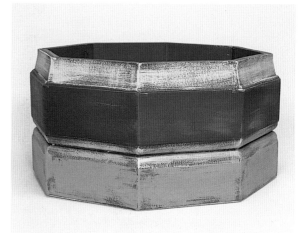

1 Apply Galaxy Blue to the lid and box bottom with a large prep brush.

2 Using the dry-brushing technique, apply the following banding colors to the bottom of the box: Nimbus Grey on the top rim, Deep Plum on the top third of the box, Pale Gold Metallic in the middle and a mix of Celadon + Pacific Blue to overlap along the bottom edge of the box.

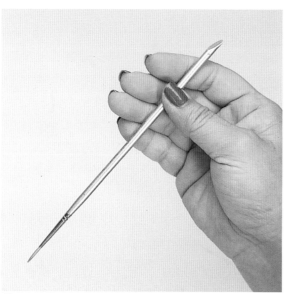

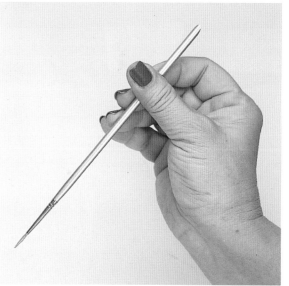

3 Use the *rock 'n' roll* technique to paint the border vines. Hold the no. 2 round near the end of the handle as this photo shows.

4 Roll the brush handle back and forth between the thumb and the fingers for the rocking motion.

Vines & Leaves

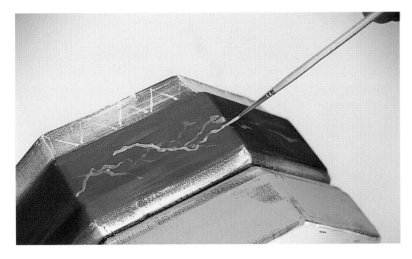

5 Put diagonal **V** stripes on the bottom rim of the box with Smoked Pearl. Next, drag a Pale Gold Metallic-loaded brush across the dark portion of the box bottom as you *rock 'n' roll*, creating a casual, spontaneous vine effect.

6 Make one-stroke leaves in a variety of sizes. The harder the pressure on the brush, the larger your leaves will be.

7 Dress a ¾-inch (19mm) glaze brush in Purple Madder, and dry-brush along the edges for an antiquing effect.

Preparing the Lid

8 Premoisten the lid with a thin coat of retarder. Working counterclockwise around the lid, apply Pacific Blue in a slip-slap manner.

9 Continue working counterclockwise with a dirty brush, from the Pacific Blue to Celadon. Blend the Celadon edge into the Pacific Blue edge.

10 Apply Brilliant Violet with overlapping strokes into neighboring colors in order to soften edges.

11 Apply a mix of Vermilion + Brown Earth (1:1) to your dirty brush, and soften into the general area of the elf's face, hat and beard.

Santa & Elves

12 Allow the surface to air dry, or speed things up with a warm hair dryer. Transfer the pattern with gray graphite paper and a stylus.

Load a no. 8 filbert with Dolphin Blue + a touch of Smoked Pearl, and shape the moon into a fuzzy-edged ball with casually brushed pit-pats. Next, add a slightly lighter value in the same manner. Begin your application in the center of the round shape, and softly walk the color out to the edges.

13 Brush sketch the santa and elves design with a no. 2 round loaded with Purple Madder. Shade all areas for contour and depth.

Tee-Hee Tip

Don't forget to add Clear Glazing Medium to all these paints for transparency!

Santa & Elves, *continued*

14 Use Purple Madder to make border branches in the same way you did the *rock 'n' roll* box border. Add very fine Carbon Black branches across the face of the moon.

15 Load your brush with a very thin mix of Brown Earth + Clear Glazing Medium and paint one-stroke border leaves. Add a few darker leaves in Purple Madder. Dab highlights of Provincial Beige on the leaves and branches.

16 Next, moisten your surface with retarder. Load a small round brush with Nimbus Grey + a touch of Clear Glazing Medium and apply **C**- and **S**-strokes for the hair, eyebrows, beard and mustache. These base strokes are broad and translucent. Add a few short wispy eyelashes, slightly overlapping the eyes.

Next, use Smoked Pearl slightly left of center in the mustache and beard. For detail, use a fine liner loaded with Smoked Pearl + Titanium White.

Base the elves' clothing with Celadon. Stroking the color from the highlights to the shading, allow the dark background to dominate the shaded areas.

Build lighter and warmer hues gradually in smaller areas with a mix of Celadon + Yellow Light (1:1) and a touch of Titanium White.

17 Lightly brush in the wings with Celadon. Next, stipple tiny dots of Nimbus Grey and Smoked Pearl with the 10/0 liner. This adds a touch of magic to the wings.

Roughly sketch in the book with Purple Madder, allowing a lot of background color to peek through. Next, highlight the book edges in Burgundy + a touch of Vermilion using very streaky dry-brushed strokes along the bookbinding. Streak Nimbus Grey + a touch of Smoked Pearl on the book pages.

Use Celadon to drybrush Santa's gloves in very faintly.

Santa Face & Elves

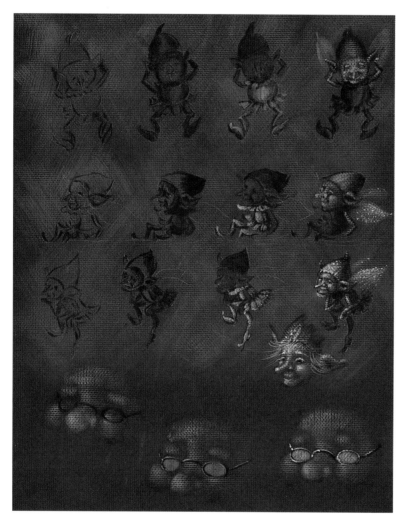

18 The first flesh mix for the Santa and elf faces is Vermilion + Brown Earth (1:1). Next, lighten with a mix of Vermilion + Brown Earth + Smoked Pearl (1:1:1) and then again with a mix of Vermilion + Yellow Light + Titanium White (1:1:1). Use Vermilion + Burgundy (1:1) to put blush on the cheeks, bottoms of noses, lips, foreheads, ears and arms.

Base the eyes in Purple Madder. Highlight Santa's eyes with a touch of Nimbus Grey.

Paint the hats Brown Earth, and then shade with the dirty brush + Purple Madder. Highlight the front edges of the hats with Raw Sienna + a touch of Yellow Light + Titanium White.

For the hair, use the flesh mix and then go over it with a no. 2 round brush loaded in Nimbus Grey, using **S**- and **C**-strokes.

For Santa's glasses, use a Brown Earth liner to outline the frame shape, and then shade the right side and bottom of the frame with Purple Madder + Carbon Black (1:1). Next, highlight the top and left of the frame in Yellow Light + a touch of Smoked Pearl. Finally, drybrush Pacific Blue on the upper left half of the glass and Brilliant Violet on the bottom of the right half. Then highlight the center of the glass area with a diagonal dry-brushing of Yellow Light + a touch of Titanium White.

Final Touches

19 "Dance" final touches of detail linework around the painting in Provincial Beige + Smoked Pearl.

20 Darken the lid edges with a dry-brush antiquing in Deep Plum + a touch of Clear Glazing Medium. I like to use the duster natural bristle brush. The trick is to fully load the brush and unload the brush tip before proceeding. Simply stroke or pounce the brush tip on the palette or a dry paper towel.

Resources

CHROMA, INC.

205 Bucky Dr.
Lititz, Pa 17543
(800) 257-8278
www.chroma-inc.com

J.W., ETC.

2205 First Street, Suite 103
Simi Valley, CA 93065
(805) 526-5066
www.jwetc.com

COUNTRY PLEASURES

Donna & Max Crews
9350 North Spring Valley Dr.
Pleasant Hope, MO 65725
(417) 759-7839
ctypleasures@getatlas.com

ROYAL & LANGNICKEL BRUSHES

6707 Broadway
Merrillville, IN 46410
(800) 247-2211

DESIGNS BY BENTWOOD, INC.

170 Big Star Dr.
P. O. Box 1676
Thomasville, BA 31792
(912) 226-1223

JO SONJA'S INC.

P.O. Box 9080
Eureka, CA 95501
(707) 455-9306
www.josonja.com

Index

Discover the Joys of Decorative Painting!

Blend the realism of fine art with the charm of decorative painting to create wildlife art that roars with life. Nine full-color, step-by-step projects provide the guidance you need to get started-everything from close-up photos and color swatch charts to growth diagrams for fur and feathers. Whether painting blue jays and tree squirrels or Siberian tigers and baby bobcats, you'll find a variety of projects that are sure to please.

ISBN 1-58180-159-9, paperback, 128 pages, #31908-K

Learn to paint your favorite Christmas themes, including Santas, angels, elves and more, on everything from glittering ornaments to festive albums with these nine all-new, step-by-step projects from renowned decorative painter, John Gutcher. He makes mastering those tricky details simple with special tips for painting fur, hair, richly textured clothing and realistic flesh tones. Just follow along with John to create a range of wonderful holiday heirlooms.

ISBN 1-58180-105-X, paperback, 128 pages, #31794-K

Fill your home with the timeless charm of folk art scenes! Popular instructors Judy Diephouse and Lynn Deptula team up to show you how to capture the quaint and picturesque beauty of rolling farmland, old-fashioned barns, churches and country gardens. You'll find ten projects for adorning everything from wooden boxes and mitten chests to picnic baskets and lampshades. Easy-to-trace patterns, paint color charts and start-to-finish instructions make each project a joy to create.

ISBN 1-58180-117-3, paperback, 128 pages, #31813-K

Painting fruits and berries is easy with the help of Priscilla Hauser, the "First Lady" of decorative painting. She shows you how to capture the colors and textures of all your favorites, including lemons, strawberries, pears, plums, blackberries, holly, pine sprigs and mistletoe. Nine fully illustrated step-by-step projects will teach you how to paint fruits and berries on everything from tin canisters and bowls to wheelbarrows, candles and more!

ISBN 1-58180-070-3, paperback, 128 pages, #31684-K

These books and other fine North Light titles are available from your local art & craft retailer, bookstore, online supplier or by calling 1-800-289-0963.